MW01036859

I BURNED FOR YOUR PEACE

PETER J. KREEFT

I BURNED FOR YOUR PEACE

Augustine's *Confessions* Unpacked

IGNATIUS PRESS SAN FRANCISCO

Cover art:
Saint Augustine
Phillipe de Champaigne (17th century)
Created between circa 1645 and circa 1650
Los Angeles County Museum of Art
Gift of The Ahmanson Foundation
Wikimedia Commons Image

Cover design by Enrique J. Aguilar Pinto

© 2016 by Ignatius Press, San Francisco
All rights reserved
ISBN 978-1-62164-040-0
Library of Congress Control Number 2015948592
Printed in the United States of America ♾

Contents

Introduction to This Book

A book about another book? Yes, for this other book is only the most beloved book in the world, next to the Bible. But why does it quote only snippets, only parts of the *Confessions*, in fact less than 10 percent of the text? Because a commentary on the whole book would be much too long. And also because we remember only snippets, we cherish only "the big ideas". To hammer those few big nails deeper into our minds is much more memorable than to tap gently at every page.

So this book is not a complete scholarly commentary on the *Confessions*. It is not complete, it is not scholarly, and it is not even a "commentary" in the usual sense of the word. It is an unpacking of some of the riches in Augustine's massive treasure chest. It is a string of pearls obtained by diving expeditions into the oyster beds in the deep sea of the *Confessions*. It is a festooning of some of the branches of the gigantic Christmas tree Augustine grew. It is a framing of some of the masterpieces of art in Augustine's studio. My words are only the unpacking, the stringing, the festooning, the framing. They set off and call attention to Augustine's words (printed in boldface type), as his words do the same thing to *the* Word, Christ. The reader must practice sign reading: look not *at* signs, but *along* them, at what they point to: look along my words to Augustine's and along his to Christ.

Here is the best way to read this book. (1) First, read each boldface-type quotation from Augustine. (2) Next, do not rush on to my commentary, but think about what Augustine said. (3) Then read what I say about it. (4) Then go back to the Augustine quote and read it in that light. Of these four stages, only one (no. 3) is from my mind. One is from yours (no. 2), and two are from Augustine's. That is the right proportion.

Introduction to Augustine

You have never met a man like Augustine. For there has never been another man like Augustine.

Medieval statues of him have many different faces but always the same two symbols: a burning heart in one hand and an open book (the Bible) in the other. For Augustine combined fire and light, a passionately fiery heart and a dazzlingly brilliant head, as no mere man in history has ever done. Saint Paul, Pascal, Dostoyevsky, Nietzsche, and Kierkegaard are the only ones I can think of who come close.

Every person now alive would be a different person, or would not be at all, if Augustine had not lived. Almost single-handedly he forged the medieval mind. Yet he is also quintessentially modern: introspective, emotional, self-doubting, complex.

He is also the major bridge between Catholics and Protestants. No other writer outside the Bible is so deeply loved and "claimed" by both "sides". He is a man for all sides, all sects, and all sexes. (Most of the lovers of Aquinas are men; half the lovers of Augustine are women.)

He lived (A.D. 354–430) during the troubled transition time that marked the end of one era and the beginning of another: between ancient and medieval, classical and Biblical, pagan and Christian, Roman and "barbarian". He lived through the Fall of Rome (A.D. 410) and died as the smoke and fires of the barbarians were burning Thagaste, his home, his native city in Africa, twenty years after Rome fell. Rome was not just a city; it was "the eternal city". Rome was the empire, Rome was the West, Rome was civilization itself. The equivalent of a nuclear winter, a five-hundred-year-long "dark ages", was beginning.

To this cosmic crisis Augustine responded with one of the most powerful and radical deeds a human being can do: he wrote a book. Many books, actually, but especially two of the greatest books ever written.

One of them, the 1500-page-long *City of God*, is the world's first philosophy of history. It interprets the Fall of Rome by putting it into the largest of perspectives, surrounding it with the greatest of frames: the story of everything, the whole history of the world from the Creation to the Last Judgment. And this, in turn, is surrounded by an even greater frame: divine Providence, the eternal Mind of God, as revealed first in Sacred Scripture and then, in light of that light, in history. (For "in your light do we see light.")

Both collectively and individually, the theme of human history is revealed as the central theme of every story: the conflict between Good and Evil, between light and darkness, between Christ and Antichrist, between "Thy will be done" and "my will be done." Augustine's terms for the collective entities that embody those two choices are the "City of God" and the "City of the World" (*Civitas Dei* and *Civitas Mundi*).

We are what we love. "Two loves have made two cities", he says: "the love of God to the refusing of self has made the City of God; the love of self to the refusing of God has made the City of the World." The City of God is the invisible but real community of all those who love God as God. The City of the World is the invisible community, or non-community, of all those who love themselves or the world as their God.

("World" here, as in Scripture, means, not the planet, which the good God made, but the "world order", the historical era that fallen man made by the Fall; it is a time-word, not a space-word.)

The City of God is a co-inherence, a true community, i.e., a common-unity. It is a diversity of individuals, races, and cultures united by its common love of the one God, which love is both *for* the one God as its one ultimate end and *from* the one God as its one ultimate origin. The City of the World is not a co-inherence but an incoherence; it is not really a community, because it worships many gods.

This polytheism is not dead today but very much alive. The fact that we no longer worship the pagan Roman gods does not mean that we are not polytheists. In fact, we are more polytheistic, not less: we have as many gods as there are worshippers.

Introduction to the *Confessions*

This drama of history, this spiritual warfare, is played out socially, publicly, visibly, and collectively in *The City of God* and individually in the *Confessions*. It is the same drama.

Two dimensions of this drama are God's providential design and man's free choices, or predestination and free will, or destiny and responsibility, both of which Augustine strongly defended. For he saw them, not as contradictory, but as complementary dimensions of the drama—like the two dimensions of every smaller story ever told by anyone *in* this Great Story: the predestination and providence of its Author and the real choices of His characters. One author could conceivably destroy or diminish a rival author's free will (e.g., by murder or a lawsuit), and one character can do the same to another character, but the author and his characters are not rivals. Therefore, predestination and free will are not rivals.

We make free choices first of all with our "heart". The "heart" is the faculty by which we love. Thus "two loves have made two cities." *Amor meus, pondus meum*, Augustine says: My love is my "weight", my gravity, my density, and therefore my destiny. I go where my love goes. To live is to love, and to love is to choose one fork in life's road rather than the other, and that choice creates your destiny. Eastbound roads simply cannot take you west, or vice versa; and

Hell-bound roads simply cannot take you to Heaven, or vice versa.

This drama is the content of time. Its end is eternity. Nothing can be more dramatic than that. *The City of God* is that drama collectively, publicly, and externally; the *Confessions* is the same drama individually, privately, and inwardly.

The *Confessions* has been the single most read, reread, and quoted post-Biblical Christian book ever written. On its very first page is the single most quoted post-Biblical Christian sentence ever written, and that sentence is its central theme and the main thing Augustine is "confessing": that "Thou hast made us for Thyself and [therefore] our hearts are restless till they rest in Thee." The *Confessions* is simply the Gospel; it is the Gospel of the restless heart.

Augustine wrote the book in the form of a prayer. It is written to God; we are allowed to overhear the conversation. That is why it is so searingly, ruthlessly honest, like the prayers of Job as distinct from the preachy platitudes of his three "friends". It is written face to face with the Face, with Light, with Omniscience.

That is also why it is so full of questions. Questions are a primary kind of "confession", viz., confessions of ignorance. The *Confessions* has more interrogative sentences in it than any other Great Book that is not in literal dialogue form. These questions are not rhetorical; they are real. And they are not mere mental curiosity: they come from the heart. They *bleed.*

The *Confessions* is also laced with hundreds of quotations from Scripture (printed in italics). For Scripture was more than an *object* of Augustine's knowledge and belief; it had become a part of the subject, the writer himself. It was not just a book but the eyes through which all books, and life itself, were read. Augustine did this as naturally as he breathed. He didn't have to "look up" verses. Scripture had become literally the very air his soul breathed.

So what does Augustine "confess"? He has the reputation of having been the playboy of the Western world; but if you are looking for juicy sex scenes you will be disappointed. What he confesses is, most fundamentally, *God* and His goodness, not just himself and his badness. This book is not first of all the story of what Augustine did about God but the story of what God did about Augustine.

To "confess" means simply to stand in the light, to will the truth, the whole truth, and nothing but the truth, especially the truth that God knows absolutely everything about you. Augustine, I'm sure, passionately loved Psalm 139, the one that celebrates the fact that "O LORD, you have searched me and known me! You know when I sit down and when I rise up." That was the very thing that Nietzsche confessed he could not endure, the deepest reason for his atheism. I think if Augustine and Nietzsche ever met, they would deeply understand each other.

Introduction to Reading the *Confessions*

There is a qualification for reading the *Confessions*. Augustine says that many will not "get" it because "they have not their ear at my heart, where I am what I am." You need not share Augustine's mind and beliefs to understand this book, but you do need to share his heart. Head-to-head scholarship is fine, if it is for the sake of heart-to-heart understanding; if not, it is dust in the eyes when reading the *Confessions*.

The experience of reading the *Confessions* feels like listening to a symphony or like tasting the world's best wine. It sings. It cries. It shouts. It whispers. It weeps. It bleeds. So does your soul if you dare to step into its words, as you would step into the sea when it is alive with waves.

It should be read as poetry is read: aloud, slowly, thoughtfully, and repeatedly. It is not a pill to be swallowed but a cud to be chewed. For it is literally inexhaustible. It is like an enormous cow that gives you fresh milk every day.

No one ever wrote words that sing like his. They fly off the page like birds. They shoot through the air like arrows of fire and shatter your heart and stun your mind. He is the greatest master of Latin who ever lived, and Latin is probably the most beautiful language that ever lived. (Yes, languages do live, and Latin is *not* "a dead language".)

I have used Frank Sheed's translation because it is an

absolute masterpiece.[1] It makes all others sound wooden and dead. (One of them was actually done by a man named Pine-Coffin!) Augustine's Latin is really poetry, and it is impossible to translate poetry faithfully out of its original language into another. Sheed has done the impossible.

[1] Augustine, *Confessions*, trans. F. J. Sheed, 2nd ed. (Indianapolis and Cambridge: Hackett, 2006). Citations supplied in parentheses after quotations include the book/chapter/paragraph number of the *Confessions* and the page number of this edition.

The "Inside Address": "Dear God,"

Augustine begins, not with narrative, but with dialogue—dialogue with God, not with us. That is the point of the whole book. That is not a clever rhetorical device, or a trick, or fluff. There is absolutely no fluff in this book.

> ***Great art Thou, O Lord, and greatly to be praised; great is Thy power, and of Thy wisdom there is no number.* And man desires to praise Thee. . . .** [This] **tiny part of all that Thou hast created . . . desires to praise Thee.** (1/1/1, p. 3)

The first and last sentences of the autobiographical narrative of the *Confessions* (the last three chapters, 11–13, are a philosophical speculation about time, eternity, and creation) are essentially the same: the book begins and ends with praise. The last sentence of book 10 is: "*they shall praise the Lord that seek Him*". It matches the first sentence of book 1. Praise connects temporal man with the eternal God, who is Alpha and Omega, the beginning and the end of time and of man; therefore praise is Augustine's beginning and his end.

Since the *Confessions* begins and ends with praise, it begins and ends with the heart, since praise comes only from the heart, the same source from which love comes. Indeed, praise is a kind of love, a part of love, a deed of love, an effect of love, or a revelation of love; we never praise anyone or anything we do not love.

Romeo praises Juliet more than he praises his own family because he loves her more. He praises his family more than Juliet's family because he loves them more. He praises his city more than any other city because he loves it more. And we—do we praise our Lord and Savior more than we praise ourselves or our friends or our favorite sports team? If Christ were here to observe our praise, would He say about us what He said about His apostles, that they were so full of irrepressible praise that "if these were silent, the very stones would cry out" (Lk 19:40)? If the answer is No, that tells you why you are not an apostle and a saint, and why eleven others, who were just like you in every other way, were.

Thomas Day wrote a funny and insightful book entitled *Why Catholics Can't Sing*. He mentioned a number of historical excuses: most American Catholic parishes are primarily Irish or Italian, and the Irish dared not sing Catholic hymns because the British would hear them and jail them, while the Italians are silent because they expect to hear opera performed in their churches. But I think he missed the heart of the answer. It's not that we can't sing, but we won't. Heads and hands don't sing, only hearts. Where do you hear singing? In Pentecostal or old Presbyterian or high Anglican or "low" Baptist churches. At Franciscan University, they sing—the same sappy hymns that Catholic congregations are too embarrassed or bored to sing elsewhere. They are the stones. We are the silent.

To praise Thee is his joy. For Thou hast made us for Thyself and our hearts are restless till they rest in Thee. (1/1/2, p. 3)

Here it is: one of the greatest sentences ever written, the basic theme of this book and of life itself.

It has two parts. The first is the objective fact, and the second is the subjective experience. In fact, the first is the fundamental objective fact of life, and the second is the fundamental subjective experience of life. They are connected by an implied "therefore": our hearts are restless until they rest in God *because* He has made us for Himself. We feel like homing pigeons because we are. Thus the fundamental claim of Christian anthropology (that God has made us for Himself) explains the fundamental fact of human experience (that our hearts are restless). The hypothesis is confirmed by the data.

There are three truths here:

(1) "To praise Thee is his joy", *for*
(2) "Thou hast made us for Thyself", *and*
(3) "Our hearts are restless till they rest in Thee."

They are related logically by the "for" and by the "and", which implies "and therefore". The fact (2) that God has made us for Himself is the fundamental objective fact. The other two statements are the two subjective experiences that follow from it and are explained by it (and by it alone): (1) that the human heart finds joy (not just pleasure or even happiness, but *joy*) in praising God, the God it has found; and (3) that it finds only restlessness without Him. Thus the deepest fact of Christian theological anthropology explains the two deepest facts of human experience.

The "for" in the first part is the English translation not of *pro* but of *ad*. "Fecisti nos *ad* te." *Pro* is the preposition for *ownership*, and if Augustine had written *pro*, the sentence still would have been profoundly true: God our Creator owns us, rightly claims us. But *ad* makes a deeper point. It is a preposition expressing dynamic movement. It means "toward". God has made us *toward* Himself. We exist "to" or "toward" or "in movement to" Him, like arrows moving toward a target or homing pigeons flying home. We are verbs as well as nouns. We are not static objects, but dynamic, moving subjects. We are not God's property so much as God's lovers. He is not only our origin and our owner, He is also our end, our purpose, our destiny, our identity, our meaning, our peace, our joy, our home. The story of Augustine's life is the story of a homeless person's journey to his true home.

And when he arrives, he finds both His own identity and God's. The two always go together, because the only place Hamlet could find his true identity would be in Shakespeare, and if Hamlet did ever find Shakespeare, he would necessarily find his own true identity.

In his *Soliloquies*, which are imaginary conversations between God and himself, Augustine imagines God asking him what he wants to know, and he replies that he wants to know only two things: who he is and who God is. "Nothing else?" God asks. "Nothing else", Augustine replies.

For everything else is relative to these two things. Everything else is *between* these two, as Jacob's ladder is between Jacob and God, between earth and Heaven. God and myself are the only two realities I can never escape for a single moment, in time or in eternity; that is why the one absolutely essential thing is to know both. And they are a package deal; neither can be known without the other also being known. Therefore the *Confessions* is *simultaneously* the story of Augustine's search for himself and his search for God.

And it is only Christ who shows us both, who reveals God to man and man to himself by being both perfect God and perfect man.

Ultimately, of course, it is God's search for Augustine. His search for God is a function of God's search for him, not vice versa. As the old hymn says,

> I sought the Lord and afterward I knew
> He moved my soul to seek Him, seeking me.
> It was not I that found, O Savior true,
> no, I was found by Thee.

Elsewhere Augustine imagines God saying to him, "Take heart; you would not be seeking Me if I had not already found You."

The "restless heart" is the very heart of every human heart. What makes Augustine different is only that he is honest enough to admit it and passionate enough to run rather than stroll through it.

This restlessness is the second most precious thing in the world, since it is the means to the only good that is even greater than itself, namely, the rest that comes only in God. Our homelessness, our alienation, our misery, our confusion, our lover's quarrel with the world—this is our greatest blessing, next to God Himself. For if it did not exist, no one would ever go to Heaven. If the baby were not restless in the womb, it would never be born. It would die. It is not better to travel hopefully than to arrive, but it is the next best thing.

> **And, *they shall praise the Lord that seek Him;* for those that seek shall find; and finding Him they will praise Him.** (1/1/2, p. 3)

Augustine here puts the three facts in a relationship of direct cause and effect: if we seek God, we will find Him (He Himself solemnly promised that, in both Testaments); and if we find Him, we will praise Him (you can't *not* praise Him when you see Him!); therefore, if we seek Him, we will praise Him.

> **Grant me, O Lord, to know which is the soul's first movement toward Thee . . . whether it must know Thee before it can implore. For it would seem clear that no one can call upon Thee without knowing Thee, for if he did he might invoke another than Thee, knowing Thee not. Yet may it be that a man must implore Thee before he can know Thee?** (1/1/2, p. 3)

You don't expect this. After the upbeat, confident, satisfying profundities we just read, the last thing you expect is a curious, dissatisfied question. But Augustine is never satisfied, as a lover is never satisfied, even when he is most satisfied. Augustine is the Christian Socrates, always asking questions, even when he is the most pious. For questioning is not impious. Jesus never once berated His disciples for asking questions.

What does he want to know? How to begin, of course. Since God has made us "toward" Himself, we must know "which is the soul's first movement toward Thee". Is it seeking God ("imploring", asking), or is it knowing what to seek? How can we seek a thing if we don't know what it is? How can we look for something if we don't know what we are looking for? But if we already know what it is, why do we *seek* to know it?

In his dialogue the *Meno*, Plato raises a similar question

about timeless truths: Do we already know them when we seek them? If not, how can we know what to seek? If so, why seek? Plato's answer is that all of us do already know the most important truths (timeless truths, Platonic Forms) innately, on an unconscious level; we just have to raise it to consciousness by philosophical questioning. If Plato is right here, if there must be a knowledge of X already in us, at least unconsciously, to guide us in our search, as a kind of confused memory of something we have lost, then this unconscious *knowledge* must come first, and *seeking* is second. Since knowledge is a work of the mind or intellect, while seeking is a work of the will or the heart, this means that the intellect is first. This is the Rationalism typical of Greek philosophy (Socrates, Plato, Plotinus, even Aristotle, who said that "man's rational self is his true self").

But for Augustine, steeped in the Bible, it is not the intellect but the heart that is the heart of man and the beginning of everything else. Solomon writes: "Keep your heart with all vigilance; for from it flow the springs of life" (Prov 4:23). And in Scripture, the "heart" is not only the heart of man but also the heart of God. For Scripture says God is love (1 Jn 4:8), and love is of the heart. Scripture also says that God is all-knowing, but it does not say God is knowledge itself (though Christ does say "I am the truth"). But it does say that "God *is* love [itself]."

This primacy of the heart and love explains why Augustine's search for God, like Job's, is expressed, not in a philosophical treatise about God, but in a prayer to Him. All of the *Confessions* is a prayer, a dialogue, a personal confession *to* God. If we "practice the presence of God" (the great title of Brother Lawrence's great little book), that is, if we conform our souls to objective reality, we will not just theologize, but we will pray; in fact, we will "pray constantly" (1 Thess 5:17)—as Augustine does. We will talk *to* God, not just *about* Him—though we will also talk about Him, just as we talk about our human lover as well as to him. Prayer is what Augustine does habitually and ubiquitously. God does not come into Augustine's book much in the third person ("He"); rather, he comes first of all, and ubiquitously, in the second person ("You"). And this is how He must come into our lives as well. Scripture tells us to "pray constantly" but not to "theologize constantly". The Devil is probably a brilliant theologian, but he never prays.

So when Augustine follows his great sentence about the "restless heart" with the prayer "Grant me, O Lord, to know which is the soul's first movement toward Thee", that is not rhetoric or fluff or playing the part of proper piety. (There is absolutely no rhetoric or fluff or part-playing in the *Confessions*.) He means it.

And he really expects an answer! Only when the one with whom you talk is deaf or dumb or dead or doesn't give a damn about you, do you *not* expect an answer. Let's not insult God by not expecting an answer, for He does not lack ears, tongue, blood, or heart. And that's not a mere metaphor or analogy; *our* ears, tongue, blood, and heart are the analogies.

And because Augustine expects an answer, he gets one. And so will we.

(1) **But how can I call unto my God, my God and Lord? For in calling unto Him, I am calling Him to me: and what room is there in me for my God, the God who made heaven and earth? Is there anything**

> **in me, O God, that can contain You? All heaven and earth cannot contain You for You made them, and me in them.**
>
> (2) **Yet, since nothing that is could exist without You, You must in some way be in all that is** [therefore also in me, since I am]. **And if You are already in me, since otherwise I should not be, why do I cry to You to enter into me? . . . O God, I should be nothing, utterly nothing, unless You were in me—**
>
> (3) **or rather unless I were in You, *of whom and by whom and in whom are all things.*** (1/2/2, pp. 3–4)

Augustine's dilemma here ((1) vs. (2)) is not just a clever logical puzzle. It is a real, lived problem. It is an apparent obstacle to the greatest of all goals, union with God, the meaning of life, the satisfaction of the restless heart. How can I say "Kumbaya" ("come by here") to God? It's like a flea saying that to an elephant. For we can't hope to possess God, as we can possess food or wealth. He can't come into us. He's too big, and we're too small. That's the point of Augustine's first paragraph, above. And the point of the second one is that it seems we can't hope to succeed on our journey on this road to God because there is no road; we are already at Destination God, since God must be already present in all things and therefore in us, for God is the One who maintains everything in being. We are like fish searching for the sea.

So here is Augustine's dilemma: If God is outside us, we have no hope of ever getting Him inside, since He is too big; and if He is already inside, there is also no point to asking Him to come to where He already necessarily is. No change, no progress, no hope seems possible.

Now Augustine could have solved this problem by making a relevant philosophical distinction: the distinction between His ontological presence to our *being*, which is necessary and already present, and His personal and moral presence to our *life*, which must be freely chosen. Or he could have distinguished our natural life (*bios*), which all men have by birth, and our supernatural life (*zoe*), which only the saved have, by faith and baptism. And he will indeed make these distinctions elsewhere in his writings. But here, he makes an even more fundamental point.

His solution, in the third paragraph, is to reverse the false assumption common to both of the two horns of the dilemma: that God must be either outside us or inside us. The perspective is wrong. In asking whether God is outside us or inside us, we are using ourselves as the touchstone, the standard, the absolute, and therefore dividing all things into what is outside (i.e., outside of *us*) or inside (i.e., inside of *us*).

Frequently in the *Confessions*, as in the Bible, God corrects the perspective that we assume in our questions rather than simply answering our questions. We assume the role of "I" and search for Him as our "Thou", our "You". But when He appears, He asserts: "I AM—I am the I and you are the you, not vice versa. I am not an ingredient in your religious experience; you are an ingredient in Mine. I am the subject, and you are My object, not vice versa. I draw the real lines between 'inside' and 'outside', not you. You are either in Me, and part of the *Civitas Dei*, or outside Me, and part of the *Civitas Mundi*."

In other words, theocentrism must replace anthropocentrism. Anthropocentrism is a typically modern error; that is one of the many reasons why Augustine is so relevant today. His sexual addiction, of course, is another one. And a third is his struggle to rise above his feelings *and* his reasonings. These are all typically modern problems, not typically ancient or medieval ones.

Ancient pagans were cosmocentric: their gods were in the cosmos. Modern secularists are anthropocentric: their God is relative to their religious experience and needs. Christians, Jews, and Muslims are theocentric: the cosmos and Man are relative to God. This is evident in the new names. The "cosmos" becomes the "creation", and Man becomes God's "creature" and "image".

This is one of many places where Augustine heals us because he does not merely show us the solutions, he also shows us our problems and struggles and errors. Most premodern writers do not show us the second. Most modern writers do not show us the first.

> **But if You fill heaven and earth, do they contain You? Or do You fill them, and yet have much over since they cannot contain You? Is there some other place into which that overplus of You pours that heaven and earth cannot hold? Surely You have no need of any place to contain You. . . . It is true that all things cannot *wholly* contain You: but does this mean that they contain part of You? . . . But are there in You parts greater and smaller? Or are You not in every place at once in the totality of Your being, while yet nothing contains You wholly?** (1/3/3, p. 4)

Augustine is not finished with this problem (or rather mystery) of God's omnipresence. If God both fills and transcends all things, how can we imagine this? Is the created universe a small part of Him? That is pantheism. The ancient Hindu *Vedas* picture the supreme God (called there "Purusha", later "Brahman") this way: "all that is made is the lower quarter of Purusha, from the knees down; the other three-quarters are Purusha Himself, in Heaven." But this is wrong. The imagination misleads us. It is designed for material things alone. Unlike all material things, God is "in every place at once in the totality of Your being", so that He does not "contain" things as a stomach contains food. Nor does anything contain Him. God is literally unimaginable. Love and knowledge are also unimaginable. Even our own souls, though finite, are unimaginable. Personal, spiritual *presence* transcends the laws and limits of material *containing*. A lot of nonsense could be avoided in contemporary "philosophy of mind" if this principle were only remembered. The answer to the question "How can we imagine this?" is that we can't. So don't try.

Once Augustine realizes that God transcends both horns of this dilemma and appears as a paradox only to the mind that implicitly denies His transcendence, he applies this principle to many other paradoxes about God, so that our either/ors become His both/ands:

> **What then is my God? . . .**
> **most merciful and most just,**
> **utterly hidden and utterly present,**
> **most beautiful and most strong . . . ,**
> **suffering no change and changing all things:**
> **never new, never old, making all things new, . . .**
> **ever in action, ever at rest,**
> **gathering all things to Thee and needing none; . . .**
> **ever seeking though lacking nothing.**
> **Thou lovest without subjection to passion,**
> **Thou art jealous but not with fear . . .**
> **angry yet unperturbed by anger.** (1/4/4, pp. 4–5)

No material things can attain these paradoxical both/and transcendences. Material things are

either hidden, because absent, or visible, because present;

either beautiful, because exquisite, or strong, because gross;

either unmoving, because not moved by another being, or moving another being and therefore itself moving, because to move something else, a material thing must itself move;

either new or old, because defined by time; and in time everything that makes new things (like a parent having children) must itself eventually grow old;

either in action or at rest, either "dynamic" or "static", either hurrying like lava or frozen like ice;

and on the personal level,

either merciful, by not giving what is deserved but therefore negating justice; or just, in giving what is deserved but therefore negating mercy (God solved that one on Calvary, where we got the mercy and He got the justice);

either seeking, and therefore needing; or not needing, and therefore not seeking;

either loving, and therefore passionate, or dispassionate, and therefore unloving;

either jealous, and therefore fearful; or fearless, and therefore uncaring;

either incapable of anger, because incapable of perturbation; or angry and therefore perturbed.

And with all this, what have I said, my God and my Life and my sacred Delight? What can one say when he speaks of Thee? (1/4/4, p. 5)

The most brilliant theologian who ever lived called his unfinished *Summa Theologiae* "straw". (Straw was used in his day to cover animal dung.) Pascal said that all philosophy is not worth a half hour's trouble. Job called the world's greatest poetry about evil (his own) "empty-headed words". The reason, in all three cases, was the same: they saw God. In His sea, our ships are only paper, and sink.

You, too, have a right to call philosophy and theology insulting names like this—after you have written the philosophy and theology Aquinas, Pascal, and Job wrote.

Yet woe to them that speak not of Thee at all. (1/4/4, p. 5)

Another dilemma transcended: we must either speak or be silent, but woe is pronounced on both speech and silence. Best is the speech that comes from silence, from the presence of the One for Whom even dumb creatures speak, the mountains dance, the hills skip like lambs, and the trees clap their hands; the One to Whom the very rocks would cry out if we do not. For He is the Word before Whose face words die and then rise again.

What art Thou to me? Have mercy, that I may tell. (1/5/5, p. 5)

This, too, is not pious rhetoric but is literally meant. In order that he may tell what God is to him, Augustine needs

God's mercy. Not only is there no hope of salvation without it, there is no hope of doing Christian philosophy or theology without it. There is no hope of writing a good spiritual autobiography without it. The secret of the power of the *Confessions* is right here. It is so simple that most scholars overlook it. It is to actually believe Him when He says: "Without Me you can do nothing" and also when He says: "Ask, and it will be given you."

> **What rather am I to Thee, that Thou shouldst demand my love and if I do not love Thee be angry and threaten such great woes?** (1/5/5, p. 5)

The theocentric reversal again! Not "what art Thou to me" but "what am I to Thee?" C. S. Lewis says he read somewhere that the most important question is what we think of God, and he replied: "By God Himself, it is not! How God thinks of us is not only more important, but infinitely more important." Charles Malik, in *A Christian Critique of the University*, said the same thing about Christian universities: that they often discuss the question what they should think about Christ, but do not dare to ask the question what Christ thinks about them.

Why does God love us so much? (How much? Look at a crucifix.) Is there any answer to that question? Thank God, there is not. For answers are always given from above downward, and there is nothing above love. Love transcends everything, even reason. When asked for its reason, love offers only itself.

Love is absurd, thank God. On the Cross, the perfect God suffers our Hell so that we rebels and sinners might enjoy His Heaven. That is really absurd! And throughout salvation history, He does not sit on His perfect, eternal, divine dignity but acts like an angry, shouting, screaming parent when He sees His children choosing paths of self-destruction. He does not confine Himself to the still, small voice, the mystic whisper. He shouts—because most of us are nearly deaf. He is utterly undignified. He lowers Himself, even before the Incarnation, to our brain-damaged level—so much so that the enemies of the Faith have a field day quoting embarrassing Old Testament divine absurdities, much as an ancient Epicurean might relish pointing out a stuffy Stoic's undignified conduct with his own children when his love gets the better of his philosophy.

> **O Lord my God, tell me what Thou art to me. *Say unto my soul, I am thy salvation.*** (1/5/5, p. 5)

But even though the question of what we are to God is greater than the question of what God is to us, the latter question is valid and necessary. And so Augustine asks it, and God answers it: "I am thy salvation." The One who reveals what God is to us is the One whose name was divinely ordained to be the answer to that question: "You shall call his name Jesus, for he will save his people from their sins" (Mt 1:21).

> **Let me see Thy face even if I die, lest I die with longing to see it.** (1/5/5, p. 5)

As another translation puts it, "Let me die, lest I die; only let me see Thy face."

That is essentially what Job said. God had told His chosen people: "Man shall not see Me and live." Moses and Job were the exceptions. But Job did not know that he would be an exception, and nevertheless he longed to see the face of God even though he thought this would mean his death.

We should all be such exceptions. And because of Christ, we will.

> **The house of my soul is too small to receive Thee: let it be enlarged by Thee. It is in ruins: do Thou repair it.** (1/5/6, p. 5)

The instruments by which you know physical things are your senses and the instruments of these instruments that expand them, like microscopes and telescopes. The instruments by which you know abstract truths (philosophy, theology, mathematics, physics) are your mind and the instruments of this instrument by which you expand it, like computers, logic, and the scientific method. But the instrument through which you know God, both in this life, "through a glass, darkly", and in the next, "face to face", is your own soul, the whole of it, especially its heart. Therefore the meaning of life is to expand your soul, by charity and the longing for God and truth, so that in Heaven it will be a larger telescope and able to see more of God. That is why God put us in time for a while rather than creating us in eternity right from the start, as He did to the angels.

> ***I contend not in judgment with Thee*, who art the truth, and I have no will to deceive myself.** (1/5/6, p. 6)

God, truth, and self are all either accepted or rejected together. To contend with God is to contend with truth, and to contend with truth is to deceive yourself. (We are very good at that, in fact much cleverer and more successful at that than at deceiving others.)

To love God is to love truth, and to love truth is to love God, at least implicitly.

To love God is to love yourself, since you are His child, made in His image; and to love yourself is to love the One in whose image you are made.

To love the light of truth is to love yourself, because truth is what you are made for, truth is the food of your soul.

This Yes or No to the light of truth is the fundamental choice. Before the Incarnation, it was only general and universal and abstract; but truth came into the world specifically and particularly and concretely in Christ. The Light that designed the world came into the world, but some men loved darkness rather than light because their deeds were evil, and they wanted to cover them up. Not Augustine. Though a sinner, he was an honest sinner. He wanted to know them and confess them. Augustine, like David, loved Psalm 139. He was *glad* God searched him and knew him, both his falling-down and his rising-up.

Perhaps Hell and Heaven are the very same thing: light, truth; but it blesses those who love it and tortures those who hate it.

> **[I]n You is no change, nor does today pass away in You. Yet in another sense in You it does pass away, for in You are all such things—they could not even have any being that could pass away unless You upheld them in being. And because Your years do not pass, Your years are today; and no matter how many our days and our fathers' days have been, they have all passed in Your undying day.** (1/6/10, p. 8)

Augustine now turns to one of his favorite topics, time. But it is not a "turn". Time is not just an abstract philosophical puzzle—though it is that too. (Augustine famously said that we all know what we mean by time as long as no one asks us, but when they do, we find out that we don't.) Time is a very practical topic. Time permeates our every dimension, spiritual as well as physical. We take time to think as well as to eat. Time is the horizon, that divides God and Man, Creator and creature. God is not in time. He is eternal, and that means, not time without beginning or ending, but full, timeless life without dead past and unborn future. God is pure life, without even the shadows of death that are pastness and futureness. Everything is present and alive to Him, including what to us is dead past or unborn future.

When he speaks about time, Augustine is not concerned with abstract, impersonal time (*kronos*), which is measured by matter moving through space, but with concrete, personal, lived time (*kairos*), with "lifetime", which is measured by souls, not by bodies; by meaning and purpose, not by spatial motion.

The *Confessions* is Augustine telling the story of his life-in-time in the presence of the eternal God, the eternal Truth, exposing the darkness of his sin to God's light and the deadness of his past to God's life. Thus his story has two dimensions, vertical and horizontal, eternal and temporal, supernatural and natural. That is why, after the (temporal) story is over, he spends three difficult books (11–13) exploring time itself and its relation to eternity, especially in God's act of the creation of time.

Notice in the quotation above how concrete and positive God is for Augustine. He does not say that God does not have "years" (i.e., life, acts, deeds); rather, he says that "Your years do not pass, Your years are today [i.e., present]." In God's "undying day", all our dying moments simply *are*, and do not pass away. Nothing is lost forever. Nothing. Here on earth we can preserve the dead past only in our memory, which is merely mental, for the real events and people of our past are past, are dead. But not in Heaven, in eternity, in God. There, then, our past *lives* in God's eternal present.

Think of the waves of the sea. Each wave is an act of the sea, and each one is different. (Any surfer knows that.) And each one, once it breaks and dies, never returns. That is history. And we are all within history, as waves are in the sea. All waves break and die. All events end. But that is not all; there is also "the rest of the story". There is another dimension. All this dying happens in a larger context: "He's got the whole world in His hands." A wave dies, but the sea that contains all waves does not. All dying happens, as everything happens, "inside" Eternal Life, for Eternal Life has no outside, except eternal death (Hell).

Attention to that eternity, that vertical dimension of life, is called religion.

The image of the waves and the sea is imperfect because it can be interpreted as pantheism. But all images are imperfect. They don't show us everything, but they do show us something.

Beginnings: Infancy

I know not where I came from, when I came into this life-in-death—or should I call it death-in-life? I do not know. (1/6/7, p. 6)

Augustine, in one of his sermons, describes our life as a rushing river that emerges from a dark, unexplorable cave called birth and disappears into another equally dark and unexplorable cave called death. Everything and everybody is being carried by this river from the one cave to the other, some sooner, some later. As Samuel Beckett puts it in *Waiting for Godot*, "They give birth astride of a grave." Or as C. S. Lewis puts it in *A Grief Observed*, "Time itself is one more name for death."

[F]or my sustenance and my delight I had woman's milk: yet it was not my mother or my nurses who stored their breasts for me: it was Yourself, using them to give me the food of my infancy, according to Your ordinance. . . . It was by Your gift that I desired what You gave and no more, by Your gift that those who suckled me willed to give me what You had given them: for it was by the love implanted in them by You that they gave so willingly that milk. . . . It was a good for them that I received good from them, though I received it not *from* them but only through

them: since all good things are from You, O God. (1/6/7, p. 6)

The first thing Augustine remembers in his life after birth is nursing. (He remembers this only vicariously, from observing other infants.) Right here, at the beginning, we find a fundamental principle of all human life, a principle about how God and creatures interact and relate. For deism, there is no interaction; God is distant. For pantheism, there is no interaction; God is the sum total of all things. For theism, there is interaction between the Creator and His creatures. And that interaction is not semi-deistic, with God stepping aside and letting us take over part of the time; nor is it semi-pantheistic, with God "helicoptering" and micromanaging and holding our hands as we draw the letters. It is the great Catholic principle of Grace Perfecting Nature, as salt perfects the different tastes of different meats and light perfects the different hues of different colors. Augustine sees the whole world as a tube: God comes in one end (His end) and out the other (our end). Everything is gift. Everything, beginning with existence itself and mother's milk. And the intermediaries who pass on the divine gifts (here, mothers) are themselves perfected by the giving, as the ministers of a king are perfected by their appointed tasks in the kingdom.

The most obvious example of this principle in the *Confessions* is Augustine's mother, Monica. The physical life that God gave Augustine through her milk is a symbol of the spiritual life God gave him through her prayers for his conversion. (That milk is a literally real "symbol", not just a concept.)

The universe is a tube through which God comes to us, in one end and out the other. Everything in life has a "from", a "through", and a "to". The "from" is God, the "to" is ourselves, and the "through" is the whole rest of the universe. Only the "from" and the "to" remain forever. The "through", He made for us in time, some fourteen billion years ago. But it is not immortal. The universe is only our placenta. When the galaxies are all dead, we will still be young, like God.

> **And when I did not get what I wanted, either because my wishes were not clear or the things not good for me, I was in a rage—with my parents as though I had a right to their submission.** (1/6/8, p. 7)

> **You made man but not the sin in him . . . *for in Thy sight there is none pure from sin, not even the infant whose life is but a day upon the earth*. . . .** [W]**hat then were my sins at that age? That I wailed too fiercely for the breast? For if today I were to make as gluttonously and as clamorously, not of course for my mother's breasts, but for the food I now eat, I should be ridiculed and quite properly condemned. This means that what I did then was in fact reprehensible, although, since I could not understand words of blame, neither custom nor commonsense allowed me to be blamed. As we grow older we root out such ways and cast them from us:** [which means that we hold them to be bad]—**for no man engaged in removing evil would knowingly cast out what is good. Surely it was not good, even for that time of life, to scream for things that would have been thoroughly bad for me; to fly into hot rage because older persons —and free, not slaves—were not obedient to me; to strike out as hard as I could, with sheer will to hurt,**

> **at my parents and other sensible folk for not yielding to demands which could only have been granted at my peril. Thus the innocence of children is in the helplessness of their bodies rather than any quality in their minds. I have myself seen a small baby jealous; it was too young to speak, but it was livid with anger as it watched another infant at the breast.** (1/7/11, pp. 8–9)

Obviously, very young children are incapable of actual sins. Augustine does not deny this. But their behavior shows the presence of Original Sin in all of us, because all of us were once infants and acted as we observe infants act: out of sheer selfishness.

Those who dislike Augustine almost always do so for one reason above others: that he believes in the reality of sin. And not only sin, but Original Sin. This is the most frequent complaint from Jews, the Eastern Orthodox, and liberal Protestants. But Original Sin simply means that we sin because we are sinners, as we sing because we are singers. It means that Christ saves us not only from the wrong in what we do but also from the wrong in what we are. It does not mean we are "totally depraved", as Calvin taught. In fact it is only because we are so good ontologically—made in God's image, holy, called to be saints—that sin is so awful: it defaces a holy masterpiece.

What we do always manifests what we are. Where else could *our* deeds come from? That is why God does not accept our lying excuses: "the devil made me do it" (Eve), or "The woman You gave me made me do it" (Adam), or "my apelike ancestry made me do it" (Darwin), or "my capitalist economy made me do it" (Marx), or "the hormones of my libido made me do it" (Freud).

As Chesterton says, Original Sin is the only Christian

dogma that is empirically verifiable merely by reading the daily newspapers. You can almost *see* Original Sin. Just look. Augustine looks and notes that our actions, from the beginning, are selfish. We are born programmed with what Freud calls "the pleasure principle": I want what I want when I want it, and I am outraged when I don't get it. We are like the seagulls in "Finding Nemo": our favorite word is "mine". That is the "original selfishness" with which we are born and from which we need to be freed—a lifelong process, definitively defeated (for most of us) only after death in Purgatory. Augustine argues, very reasonably, that we all act as if we really do believe in Original Sin even if we quarrel with the term, because we do not tolerate morally infantile selfishness in adults when we find it. And we find it everywhere. Even the greatest saints see it in themselves.

In fact, the more saintly you are, the more you see it. Are saints fools? How could it be that truth and goodness contradict each other?—that the more we change from evil to good, the more we are deceived by the illusion of Original Sin?

The Good News of the Gospel makes no sense if the Bad News of sin is denied. "Religion is a crutch", says the secular Pharisee. It is. And fools think they are not cripples.

The word "sophomore" means, literally, "wise fool". It was coined back in the days when all college students had to take philosophy courses as freshmen. They graduated from high school thinking they were big shots who knew it all. Then they studied Socrates, who said that there were only two kinds of people: the wise, who knew they were fools, and fools, who thought they were wise. By the time they were sophomores, they had grown from being foolish fools to being wise fools, like Socrates.

Jesus said something strikingly similar. He classified people into sinners who thought they were saints (Pharisees, ancient or modern) and saints who knew they were sinners. That's why, when asked to name the four cardinal virtues, Augustine replied: Humility, humility, humility, and humility. And that's why Jesus didn't just demand "Believe", but "Repent and believe."

> [I observed that] **my elders would make some particular sound, and as they made it would point at or move towards some particular thing; and from this I came to realise that the thing was called by the sound they made when they wished to draw my attention to it.** (1/8/13, p. 10)

Here Augustine points to the simplest and clearest way to distinguish Man from all the other animals: he is, as the Greeks said, "the animal who has the word" (*zoon echon logon*). For he alone is made in the image of the Word, Who was in the beginning with God and Who was God (Jn 1:1–2).

This is what Walker Percy, in his philosophical semiotics (the science of signs), calls "the delta factor" (in *Lost in the Cosmos*). For the higher animals, as for us, there is (a) the empirical world, (b) the individual consciousness, and (c) (b)'s awareness of (a). But there is in Man also a fourth dimension (delta as well as alpha, beta, and gamma), namely, language, meaningful mental signs, which cannot be reduced to any of the first three dimensions.

Helen Keller's individual breakthrough to this properly human dimension came in that great scene by the well in *The Miracle Worker*, where she realizes that the physical gesture in sign language *means* the physical water for which she thirsted. This individual breakthrough replicates the breakthrough in history from ape to man, from evolution to creation. For Man's awareness of this spiritual dimension cannot be accounted for simply by evolution from below but only by enlightenment from above.

Augustine thinks deeply about this in his *De Magistro* ("On the Teacher") and concludes that all human reason (*logos*) is a lived participation in the divine Reason, the divine Logos. This is the same point C. S. Lewis makes in *Miracles*: that therefore every act of human reason is literally a supernatural miracle. For when we understand (the first act of the rational mind) or judge (the second act) or argue (the third act), we are participating in the activity of the Word of God, the pre-incarnate eternal Christ, whom Augustine calls "the Interior Master".

When we speak, animals hear the sounds, and higher animals can follow them as signals and be trained to respond in certain ways; but they cannot understand them as signs, as meanings, as symbols. They look *at* words as things instead of looking *along* them as signs. (See C. S. Lewis' essay "Meditation in a Toolshed" for this crucial distinction.)

The essence of Deconstructionism is the reduction of human "texts" (language) to the animal level, the denial of significance or objective truth. To quote the proto-Deconstructionist poet Archibald MacLeish in "Ars Poetica", "A poem should be palpable and mute / as a globed fruit. / . . . A poem should not mean / But be." This undermines everything human. Everything. It is the most anti-human and universally destructive philosophy in the history of human thought.

At the very beginning of his life, Augustine implicitly confesses both his own essential humanity and its origin in the divinity of the Word of God, in confessing his first learning of language, his first "Helen Keller moment". This is fitting, for no philosopher has ever loved language more or used it more beautifully. Augustine's later conversion also had a linguistic dimension, for it was a conversion from thc selfish use of this great power of rhetoric for worldly gain and folly to the use of it for the glory of God.

Education

O God, my God, what emptiness and mockeries did I now experience: for it was impressed upon me as right and proper in a boy to obey those who taught me, that I might get on in the world and excel in the handling of words to gain honour among men and deceitful riches. I, poor wretch, could not see the use of the things I was sent to school to learn; but if I proved idle in learning, I was soundly beaten. (1/9/14, p. 10)

Perhaps an unbiased observer would hold that I was rightly punished as a boy for playing with a ball: because this hindered progress in studies—studies which would give me the opportunity as a man to play at things more degraded. (1/9/15, p. 11)

Augustine here begins his critique of his pagan Roman education. This is not just for autobiographical purposes. For the *Confessions* is not essentially, but only accidentally, an autobiography; it is essentially a *confession*, i.e., a prayer.

Augustine reflects on his education because all of life is education, all of culture is education. And the lessons in worldly "success" that he learned in the fourth century in his pagan culture are exactly the same lessons we learn in the twenty-first century, in our so-called Christian culture.

And what they all amount to is Ecclesiastes' "vanity of

vanities". Augustine's deepest critique is not just an ethical and moral one, that he learned to sin. It's not just that his education did not give him virtue, but that it did not give him meaning and purpose and wisdom. They were "empty". That's the key word. Augustine's human hunger for fullness, for realness, for true being, was not being met. And that ontological hunger is a God-implanted hunger. Even when that fact is not known or acknowledged, it is still in fact a hunger for Him, Who alone is true being. (As Aquinas would later formulate it, God is not just *a* being, but Being: His very essence is existence.) The thirst for God is an ontological thirst. It is the holy restlessness of the heart that was designed in Heaven and *for* Heaven and Him, not in and for Harvard or Hollywood—or Rome.

This "vanity" showed itself in the irony of a lived self-contradiction: Augustine was punished for playing instead of studying because studying was the way to "get on in the world", i.e., to get rich so that he could—do what? Play. That's like skipping meals that are available for free today so that you can buy seeds to plant food that you hope to grow and eat tomorrow. The irony is biting. It takes a very complex and sophisticated civilization to cover up such foolishness, as it takes millions of mice to cover up the elephant in the room.

Yet, Lord, I observed men praying to You: and I learnt to do likewise, thinking of You (to the best of my understanding) as some great being who, though unseen, could hear and help me. As a boy I fell into the way of calling upon You, my Help and my Refuge; and in those prayers I broke the strings of my tongue—

praying to You, small as I was but with no small energy, that I might not be beaten at school. (1/9/14, p. 11)

Augustine continues his exploration of beginnings here with the most primitive beginning of his religion, i.e., of his relationship with God. Prayer is the very life-breath of that relationship. His first prayer is very crude and childish and egocentric, of course; but it is real, and therefore he does not find it laughable, as others did.

The most primitive prayer is "Help". (Did the Beatles know how profoundly prayerful their famous title was?) "Help" is just one letter above the animal "yelp". But it is a radical step: animals do not pray.

Christ put that particular petition ("Deliver us from evil") at the *end* of His model prayer ("the Lord's prayer") rather than at the beginning, because He knew we tend to reverse the divine order in all things. Augustine, like all of us, needed to learn the other six petitions and to put them all in their proper order. He had learned that lesson well by the time he wrote the *Confessions* for he began and ended that prayer/book with "Hallowed be Thy name", i.e., with praise and adoration. Augustine, like all of us, learned very slowly and gradually, but he did learn. Once the most primitive prayer begins, once the borders of religion are crossed, God will not be satisfied until He has made a silk purse out of a sow's ear. In fact, that last sentence is a pretty good summary of the whole point of the *Confessions.* It's really about God, not about Augustine.

[T]**he one thing I revelled in was play; and for this I was punished by men who after all were doing exactly**

> **the same things themselves. But the idling of men is called business; the idling of boys, though exactly like, is punished by those same men: and no one pities either boys or men.** (1/9/15, p. 11)

> **I loved too to have my ears tickled with the fictions of the theatre. . . . Yet those who put on such shows are held in high esteem. And most people would be delighted to have their sons grow up to give similar shows in their turn—and meanwhile fully concur in the beatings those same sons get if these shows hinder study: for study is the way to the prosperity necessary for giving them! Look down in mercy, Lord, upon such things; and set us free.** (1/10/16, p. 10)

Here is the lived self-contradiction again; and God's role is not merely to judge and condemn us for it but to free us from it, because we are prisoners. Augustine prays that God free us, not from playing with balls or theaters, but from the vanity, the self-contradiction, and the hypocrisy by which adults both punish and reward children for acting like adults.

Here is also the realization that adults are only large children, who mask that fact by calling their vanity "business" and children's vanity "play". But whether it is in a ball park or in a theater, a vanity by any other name would smell as unsweet or taste as sour. Whatever is from God and for God is sweet. Everything else is sour. "Sweet" and "sour" here are metaphors for "real" and "unreal". Only what has God's fingerprints on it is real. As Chesterton put it, "One thing is needful—everything—the rest is vanity of vanities."

One of the best ways to understand adults is to study children. (This is something the ancients did comparatively little of—another way Augustine is surprisingly modern.) If you want to know why we wage wars, watch twenty unsupervised two-year-olds for twenty minutes.

> **When I was still a child, I fell gravely ill . . . and was close to death . . . but I made a sudden recovery. This caused my baptismal cleansing to be postponed: for it was argued that if I lived I should inevitably fall again into the filth of sin: and after baptism the guilt of sin's defilement would be in itself graver and put the soul in graver peril.** (1/11/17, pp. 12–13)

This is, of course, a misunderstanding of the purpose of baptism, as Augustine implies in the words "it was argued that". It treats baptism as a kind of spiritual technology or magic.

But this very misunderstanding can be instructive to our understanding, especially in our technology-idolizing culture. Technology and magic are identical in their end (power), only different in their means or power source (material vs. spiritual, natural vs. preternatural). That is why these two things flourished in the same time (the Renaissance) and place (Western civilization). The only reason the richest man in America today is a computer CEO rather than a magician is because technology was found to work more reliably than magic.

Baptism really does cleanse us from Original Sin. It is not a mere sign or symbol; it is also a reality, with power. It "effects what it symbolizes". But not impersonally, automatically, and predictably, like technology. It works personally, freely, and in unpredictable and individuated ways, like love. Like the divine grace it conveys, it uses and perfects nature rather than bypassing it, and it therefore uses human nature and the free will that is essential to human nature. This is obvious in the case of adults who freely ask for baptism; but even in infant baptism, it is the freely chosen faith, hope, and love of the infant's parents and of Mother Church that "turns on" the faucet to let the water of divine grace flow through the pipe of baptism into the soul of the infant.

> **I disliked learning and hated to be forced to it. But I was forced to it, so that good was done to me though it was not my doing. Short of being driven to it, I certainly would not have learned. But no one does well against his will, even if the thing he does is a good thing to do.** (1/12/19, p. 13)

> [F]**ree curiosity is of more value in learning than harsh discipline. But by Your ordinance, O God, discipline must control the free play of curiosity.** (1/14/23, p. 16)

Augustine's psychology of education, like so many things in Augustine, is a synthesis of premodern objectivity and modern subjectivity. The premodern, objective truth is the need for discipline in us all (for we are all fallen, foolish, and lazy students) in order to do an objectively good thing to the students even against their subjective will if necessary. This applies to God as our Teacher as well as to human teachers: we need to suffer subjectively, if necessary, to become objectively perfect (wise and good). The modern, personalist half of the truth is the importance of subjective motivation: that "free curiosity is of more value in learning than harsh discipline." For curiosity can be a form of love, the love of truth.

> **I was forced to memorise the wanderings of Aeneas —whoever *he* was—while forgetting my own wanderings; and to weep for the death of Dido who killed herself for love, while bearing dry-eyed my own pitiful state, in that among these studies I was becoming dead to You, O God, my Life.** (1/13/20, p. 14)

Augustine's complaint here is another typically modern one: the lack of what we would call existential relevance in his education. It changed his skills but not his life; his ideas but not his character. Like the theater, it was merely a spectator sport.

This critique of classical education for lacking "relevance", a critique often heard from secularists, becomes even more important from a religious perspective. For what Augustine was distracted from when he learned to weep for Dido's fictional physical dying for the love of her fictional human lover, Aeneas, was his own real spiritual dying to the love of the real divine lover, God. The irony is painfully obvious. Sin's follies are so stupid that they would be hilariously funny if they weren't so serious.

> **But** [in this matter of classical studies] **how woeful are you, O torrent of established custom. Who can resist you?** (1/16/25, p. 16)

Again, the critique is not the customary moralism we expect, but the questioning of "established custom" itself. Augustine, like ourselves, lived in a pagan culture, and therefore in order to be Christian, he had to be countercultural. Whether this is normal or even inevitable, or whether a Christian culture is possible and called for, is not the question here. Our pressing problem is practical: in our post-Christian culture, as in Augustine's pre-Christian one, we must question "established custom" and swim against the current, upstream, like salmon. Only live fish can swim upstream; dead ones can only "go with the flow". The next time you hear someone argue against Christian morality by noting that "this is the twenty-first century, not the first", remember you are listening to a dead fish.

Was not the whole business so much smoke and wind? (1/17/27, p. 18)

There is a deep significance to Augustine's choice of words here. He criticizes his education and the whole pagan society behind it and the whole "City of the World" (*Civitas Mundi*) behind that for being "smoke and wind", for its "emptiness". Why does he not say its "errors" or its "vices"? Augustine thirsts for truth and yearns to escape from both error and skepticism; but that is not his most fundamental thirst. He thirsts for goodness and yearns to escape from sin and immorality, but that is not his most fundamental thirst. He thirsts for beauty (his very first book was about that) and yearns to feast on it, but that is not his most fundamental thirst. His most fundamental thirst is his ontological thirst, the thirst for being, for reality. He longs to exchange emptiness for fullness, unreality for reality. He wants to escape error because it is the mind's fake food, the mind's unreality. He wants to escape sin because sin is the will's fake food, the will's unreality. He wants beauty for the same reason he wants truth and goodness: because it is the mark of being. For whoever has being also has truth and goodness and beauty because these are three properties of all being. Philosophers call them three "transcendentals" because they transcend particularity.

> **[I]t was no wonder that I fell away into vanity and went so far from Thee, my God, seeing that men were held up as models for my imitation who were covered with shame if, in relating some act of theirs in no way evil, they fell into some barbarism or grammatical solecism: yet were praised, and delighted to be praised, when they told of their lusts, provided they did so in correct words correctly arranged. . . . [W]ith what anxious care the sons of men observe the rules of letters and syllables . . . , while they neglect the eternal rules of everlasting salvation.** (1/18/28, 29, pp. 18–19)

This is why most modern movies, though technologically superior to old ones, are less satisfying: they are full of "bells and whistles" and empty of significance. They are what life was to Macbeth: "full of sound and fury, signifying nothing". Like Augustine's teachers, they are sticklers on technical means and indifferent to substantive ends. Their style is sophistication with little substance, and their content is lust with little love.

Childhood

> **[I]n games, when I was clearly outplayed I tried to win by cheating, from the vain desire for first place. At the same time I was indignant and argued furiously when I caught anyone doing the very things that I had done to others. When I was caught myself, I would fly into a rage rather than give way.** (1/19/30, p. 20)

How many kids never cheat? It's almost the same number as how many infants never cry. We'd rather be bad winners than good losers. We fear losing at games by not cheating more than we fear losing at life by cheating.

But at the same time we know we are doing wrong, which is why we "argue furiously" when we catch others cheating. We're very impatient when we see in others the faults we are much too patient with in ourselves. The natural law, the Golden Rule, is something that, in J. Budziszewski's words, "we can't not know", or, in Aquinas' words, "cannot be eradicated from the heart of man". That's also why we "fly into a rage rather than give way" when we are caught in our own sins. We *passionately* hate to admit we did wrong. Our very passion in refusing to confess our sin is itself an involuntary confession. As Shakespeare said, "the lady doth protest too much, methinks."

> **It is strange that we should not realise that no enemy could be more dangerous to us than the hatred with**

> **which we hate him, and that by our efforts against him we do less damage to our enemy than is wrought in our own heart.** (1/18/29, p. 19)

"Whatever a man sows, that will he also reap" (Gal 6:7). Hindus call that karma. It is true. It is the moral law of cause and effect. Every act, both good and evil, has two effects: one on its object and one on its subject. Just as every stroke of the lumberjack's axe that weakens the tree's trunk also strengthens his own muscles, every stroke of the whip that softens the victim's flesh also hardens the flogger's heart. Mother Teresa said that every abortion has two victims: the baby's body and the mother's conscience.

We know this law by experience, which is why we recognize it when we read great philosophers like Plato saying it; yet we also do not know it: we suppress it. As one great old psychologist said, we "by [our] wickedness suppress the truth" (Rom 1:18). Or, to quote another, "The light has come into the world, and men loved darkness rather than light, because their deeds were evil" (Jn 3:19). It is not just ignorance, it is ignoring. We are not only very good at being bad, but we are also very, very good at self-deception. Augustine does not spare us.

That is why reading the *Confessions* is a good rehearsal for death, judgment, and Purgatory—and, eventually, Heaven. All four of these (death, judgment, Purgatory, and Heaven) are made of light, of truth. Truth is an absolute. Even Hell is truth, known too late. The same thing that blesses the blessed in Heaven damns the damned in Hell. Truth unconfessed tortures, truth confessed blesses and blisses.

> **Is this boyhood innocence? It is not, Lord. I cry Thy mercy, O my God. Yet as we leave behind tutors and**

> **masters and nuts and balls and birds and come to deal with prefects and kings and the getting of gold and estates and slaves, these are the qualities which pass on with us, one stage of life taking the place of another as the greater punishments of the law take the place of the schoolmaster's cane.** (1/19/30, p. 20)

Augustine (1) asks the crucial diagnostic question "Is this boyhood innocence?"; (2) answers it simply and honestly (because he is speaking to God, not just to himself; he is standing in the great searchlight); (3) throws himself on God's mercy, with a desperate cry that is the only reasonable response because that mercy is our only hope; and (4) reminds us that we all are just big kids. The difference is only quantity, not quality. That's why studying children is one of the best ways to "know thyself."

> **Yet, Lord, I should have owed thanks to You . . . even if it had been Your will that I should not live beyond boyhood. For even then I was; I lived; I felt. . . .** [E]**ven that I exist is Thy gift.** (1/20/31, pp. 20–21)

I can never forget a woman I saw on TV many years ago being interviewed by an arrogant talk show host (Phil Donahue, I think) about her reasons for not choosing to have an abortion when the doctors told her, truly, that her child would not live after birth for more than a few weeks. She said, "I just wanted him to have a chance to see the sun." *Any* life is a triumph over nonbeing. "Even that I exist is Thy gift." Being given existence, i.e., being created, is a unique gift because it is given to one who does not yet even exist to receive it. No one can deserve it or have a right to it.

I know a woman whose husband died at forty-two, after only twenty-one years of marriage. Her response to his death was: "Twenty-one wonderful years!" Others saw her glass as empty because they compared it with other glasses; she saw it as full because she compared it with nothingness. The difference between twenty-one and eighty-one is only relative; the difference between twenty-one and zero is absolute. Gratitude is not only subjectively good, it is also objectively true.

Adolescence: Lust and Pears

> **Arrived now at adolescence I burned for all the satisfactions of hell, and I sank to the animal in a succession of dark lusts: my beauty consumed away and I stank in Thine eyes, yet was pleasing in my own and anxious to please the eyes of men.** (2/1/1, p. 25)

Like all the saints, Augustine's attitude toward his own sins looks extreme to us. For to the cold blooded, 98.7 degrees is a high fever. The closer we get to the Light, the darker and deeper the holes in our soul appear; and the farther away from the Light we are, the more self-satisfied we are, like Pharisees or pop psychologists. Sinners see themselves as saints; saints see themselves as sinners. Who is right? Whose eyes are the standard? The obvious answer to that question is: God is the standard. If so, Augustine is not an "extremist" or a "fanatic" at all but simply a realist.

This is not the whole story, of course, but only the "bad news". But without the bad news the good news is meaningless. A free heart transplant (which is what the Christian Gospel is) is not good news to someone who does not know he has heart disease (which is what Original Sin is).

Grace is infinitely greater than sin. The goodness of the good news is infinitely greater than the badness of the bad news. That is why the bad news must be proclaimed: for the sake of the good news. For we, unlike God, appreciate things only by contrast. (Shocking news flash: we are not God.)

Augustine mentions all three sources of sin here: the world ("to please the eyes of men"), the flesh ("I sank to the animal in a succession of dark lusts"), and the Devil ("the satisfactions of hell").

> **My one delight was to love and to be loved. But in this I did not keep the measure of mind to mind, which is the luminous line of friendship; but from the muddy concupiscence of the flesh and the hot imagination of puberty mists steamed up to becloud and darken my heart so that I could not distinguish the white light of love from the fog of lust. Both love and lust boiled within me.** (2/2/2, p. 25)

Augustine does not find himself "totally depraved", like a Calvinist. There is a profound good and wisdom mixed with his evil and folly. "My one delight was to love and be loved"—his heart is right there. But it is not true love and not a love of truth. Every time he criticizes his lust, he points to this: the lack of light, "the measure", "the luminous line". Concupiscence creates "mists" that "becloud and darken" the mind and confuse good and evil so that we cannot "*distinguish* the white light of love from the fog of lust".

Lust is not true love for three reasons. First, it is selfish: what we love is not the person but the experience. Second, it is only animal love; it does not rise to the level of reason and free will. Third, it is not subject to God and His will and does not intend to be. The fact that most people today do not clearly know this explains part of our fascination with Augustine. This "old stuff" is radically new to us.

> **But to whom am I telling this? Not to Thee, O my God, but in Thy presence I am telling it to my own kind, to the race of men, or rather to that small part of the human race that may come upon these writings. And to what purpose do I tell it? Simply that I and any other who may read may realise out of what depths we must cry to Thee.** (2/3/5, p. 27)

Augustine frequently interrupts himself to ask himself what he is doing and why he is doing it—an excellent habit to cultivate! It is before the face of God that he confesses, but also before the face of men; for although God does not need to learn anything from him, we do. We comfortable cultural conformists very badly need to learn "out of what depths we must cry to Thee." Before God can comfort the afflicted, He needs to afflict the comfortable. That is the purpose of the *Confessions*: our education in the "good news" and, therefore, also that essential part of it which is the "bad news".

> **Whose but Yours were the words You dinned into my ears through the voice of my mother, Your faithful servant? Not that at that time any of it sank into my heart. . . . Yet it was from You. . . . You were speaking to me through her, and in ignoring her I was ignoring You.** (2/3/7, p. 28)

Here again we see the principle of grace using nature, the Word of God coming to us through men, especially through women (as It came in person through Mary). Augustine's only partially dead conscience was the very Word of God coming to him from within; and the words of his mother, Monica, were the words of God coming to him from without. God usually uses these two-bladed scissors to cut into our heart. For He is performing a slow and delicate heart surgery on us. "The wounded surgeon plies the steel" (T. S. Eliot). The whole universe is God's hospital: first of all, our obstetrics ward and then, our recovery room.

> **I was ashamed among the other youths that my viciousness was less than theirs; I heard them boasting of their exploits, and the viler the exploits the louder the boasting; and I set about the same exploits not only for the pleasure of the act but for the pleasure of the boasting.** (2/3/7, p. 28)
>
> **Your law, O Lord, punishes theft; and this law is so written in the hearts of men that not even the breaking of it blots it out: for no thief bears calmly being stolen from.** (2/4/9, p. 29)

"The world" is often a more powerful temptation to lust than "the flesh". Augustine (like us) is more "ashamed to be ashamed" in the sight of his friends by not sinning with them than he is ashamed in the sight of God for sinning. Like a good Freudian, he feels guilty only about feeling guilty. Like FDR, he believed that "We have nothing to fear (or feel guilt about) but fear (or guilt feeling) itself."

Being bad is bad (unless the law of noncontradiction has been revoked—check the latest news from ninth circuit federal judges); and boasting about being good is also bad; but boasting about being bad is doubly bad.

But even the doubly bad cannot be triply bad. The natural moral law is "so written in the hearts of men that not even the breaking of it blots it out", though sometimes it is only when we are sinned against that we acknowledge, by our protest, that sin is sin. The man without any conscience at all would treat being spat on in the same way as being rained on. "Man is a machine", said La Mettrie and all the materialists who followed him; but they do not really believe that, for when the coke machine fails to deliver a coke, they do not preach to it or tell it to go to confession or put it in jail. They kick it. So far, even tyrants have not treated men that way. Even tyrants give their victims the respect of hating them. Only a man, never a machine, can rise to the dignity of sin. It's a great compliment to call a man a sinner.

> **There was a pear tree near our vineyard, heavy with fruit, but fruit that was not particularly tempting either to look at or to taste. . . . We carried off an immense load of pears, not to eat—for we barely tasted them before throwing them to the hogs. Our only pleasure in doing it was that it was forbidden. Such was my heart, O God. . . . Let that heart now tell You what it sought when I was thus evil for no object, having no cause for wrongdoing save my wrongness . . . , seeking no profit from wickedness but only to be wicked.** (2/4)

Why is this passage so famous? Certainly not because stealing pears was such a terrible sin or that Augustine thinks it is. It fascinates us because it probes a great mystery: the origin of evil, the motivation for sin. And it does this in the simple case of a child, where we can see it more clearly.

Augustine pursues this question like a cat obsessed with a mouse, because the diagnosis of any disease is the first step toward its cure. If all sin originates in an underlying something, then we must avoid that something more than death itself and cultivate its opposite. As Augustine will discover shortly, that something is variously named pride, playing God, "my will be done", and "the will to power".

Apparently, this evil deed was done simply for the sake of evil, simply because it was evil; for if the pears had not been forbidden, Augustine and his friends would not have taken them. They were not edible or saleable or enjoyable. It was only the act of stealing them, the evil act, that was enjoyable. Forbidden fruit tastes sweetest. But why? How can evil appear as good precisely because it is evil? That is both a logical and a psychological contradiction. The will can only choose some kind of good, some at least apparent good, just as the mind can only believe an apparent truth. Augustine must seek further.

> **Now when we ask why this or that particular evil was done, it is normal to assume that it could not have been done save through the desire of gaining or the fear of losing some one of these lower goods. For they have their own charm and their own beauty, though compared with the higher values of heaven they are poor and mean enough. Such a man has committed a murder. Why? He wanted the other man's wife or his property; or he had chosen robbery as a means of livelihood. . . . What was it then that in my wretched folly I loved in you, O theft of mine, deed wrought in that dark night when I was sixteen? For you were not lovely: you were a theft.** (2/5–6/11–12, p. 30)

Pure good is possible (that's God), but pure evil is not. This is true both objectively, or ontologically, and subjectively, or psychologically. As Augustine will discover much later, when he thinks his way out of the Manichean philosophy that taught that good and evil are both equally real (good being spirit or spirituality and evil being matter), evil can only be a parasite on good: moral evils presuppose ontological goods. An evil assassin's stroke has to be a good stroke of a good sword. And the same is true subjectively, psychologically. In order to tempt us to love evil, Satan has to lie, has to present each evil as some kind of good. Only an apparent good can attract our desires, even when the apparent good is really evil, just as only apparent truth can attract our mind, even when it is really a lie. When he fishes for our souls, the Devil always has to mask his nasty, cold, and deathly hook with bait: a nice, fat, lively worm.

Augustine then verifies this principle that all evils are apparent goods inductively, by examples.

> **For there is a certain show of beauty in sin.**
>
> **Thus pride wears the mask of loftiness of spirit, although You alone, O God, are high over all.**
>
> **Ambition seeks honour and glory, although You alone are to be honoured before all and glorious forever.**
>
> **By cruelty the great seek to be feared, yet who is to be feared but God alone . . . ?**
>
> **The caresses by which the lustful seduce are a seeking for love: but nothing is more caressing than Your charity. . . .**
>
> **Ignorance and sheer stupidity hide under the names of simplicity and innocence: yet no being has simplicity like to Yours: and none is more innocent than You. . . .**
>
> **Sloth pretends that it wants quietude: but what sure rest is there save the Lord?**

> **Luxuriousness would be called abundance and completeness; but You are the fullness and inexhaustible abundance of incorruptible delight.**
>
> **Wastefulness is a parody of generosity: but You are the infinitely generous giver of all good.**
>
> **Avarice wants to possess overmuch: . . . but what can excel before You?**
>
> **Anger clamours for just vengeance: but whose vengeance is so just as Yours? . . .**
>
> **Thus even those who go from You and stand up against You are still perversely imitating You. But by the mere fact of their imitation, they declare that You are the creator of all that is, and that there is nowhere for them to go where You are not.** (2/6/13–14, pp. 31–32)

The general principle Augustine finds in all these particular examples of sins is then applied to the particular sin of stealing the pears. What was the ap-pear-ant good there?

This is a very practical question. It can mean the difference between life and death for a fish to recognize and avoid the bait.

Since all good is in God, we are seeking what God is even when we sin. When the john knocks on the door of a whorehouse, he is really looking for a cathedral.

This ignorance and folly does not excuse us, of course, for we are not merely ignorant; we make ourselves ignorant; we willfully ignore God. Plato traced all evil back to ignorance, which is profoundly true as far as it goes; but Augustine traces the ignorance back one more step.

"Even those who go from You and stand up against You are still perversely imitating You." When we flee from God, we must use His power of freedom as our road. All created powers are from Him, are participations in His perfections. So all sin is a kind of sacrilege or blasphemy, for it uses God's own stuff to oppose Him. The holy powers He gave us as part of His image in us—our reason and free will—are the powers we use whenever we sin.

So since "even those who go from You and stand up against You are still perversely imitating You" (the end of the previous quotation), the question then becomes: "Of what excellence of my Lord was I making perverse and vicious imitation?" (the beginning of the next quotation). Having found his abstract, general principle, he now uses it to explain the concrete particular.

Notice how Augustine's mind habitually moves from a particular problem to a general principle and then moves from the general principle back down to the particular again. You can see the same double movement in Saint Paul's practical epistles. This may seem like a very abstract principle of logic, but it is also very practical. There is no other way to learn truth about particulars. They do not illuminate themselves; only general principles illuminate them—just as particular colors do not illuminate themselves; only light, which transcends all colors, illuminates them. We learn about universals (like light) only from particulars (like colors), and then we judge truths about particulars (like colors) only in light of universals (like light itself).

So once again what did I enjoy in that theft of mine? Of what excellence of my Lord was I making perverse and vicious imitation? Perhaps it was the thrill of acting against Your law . . . , the delight a prisoner might have in making some small gesture of liberty—getting a deceptive sense of omnipotence from

> **doing something forbidden without immediate punishment. I was that slave, who fled from his Lord and pursued his Lord's shadow.** (2/6/14, p. 32)

"I'm the boss", "I'm in charge here", "I make the rules here." That's what we want to say. It's God's power and authority that we envy. We rankle under it and long to be over it. Since we can't really, we pretend we can, like a prisoner giving his captors an obscene gesture when their backs are turned. But God has no back; He is all face.

When we see it that simply and clearly, we are embarrassed that we missed something so obvious. But the Devil does not want to let us see it that simply and clearly. God has to remind even His saints repeatedly (as He said to Saint Catherine) of the two most obvious truths of all: "I'm God and you're not."

Tolkien wrote that *The Lord of the Rings* is a deeply religious novel even though God and religion are never mentioned. He even said that God is the most important character in the story. For why is Sauron evil? Why is it evil for him to play God with his ring of unlimited power? Only because there is a God and Sauron is not God. If there was no one who had a real right to the throne, it would not be wrong for us to claim it.

> **Now—as I think back on the state of my mind then—I am altogether certain that I would not have done it alone. Perhaps then what I really loved was the companionship of those with whom I did it. . . . Someone cries, "Come on, let's do it"—and we would be ashamed to be ashamed.** (2/8–9/16–17, pp. 33–34)

Augustine is not satisfied with his first answer, however true and even profound it may be. He discovers another one:

peer pressure (which in this case was pear pressure). The good that is perverted here is "honor among thieves", i.e., friendship or companionship, which is a form of love, which is the greatest good because it is what God is. When very good things are misused and perverted, they can do very evil things. "The corruption of the best is the worst."

"Ashamed to be ashamed"—how utterly modern and American this is! Like Augustine and his teenaged friends, we are what David Riesman and Nathan Glazer, in *The Lonely Crowd*, call "other-directed" rather than either "tradition-directed" or "inner-directed". Having refused the hierarchy and authority of their shepherds ("tradition-direction"), the sheep have not become shepherds themselves ("inner-direction") but only "other-directed" sheep pretending and claiming to be "inner-directed" but really following each other around in circles of intellectual fashionableness.

Riesman and Glazer wrote *The Lonely Crowd* in 1954. Since then (I started teaching in 1962), I have found my students' politically correct opinions becoming increasingly standardized and conformist every decade, as we get closer to the "brave new world" that de Tocqueville called "soft totalitarianism". It is now fashionable to feel guilty only about feeling guilty, to be ashamed only of being ashamed.

Young Adulthood: Carthage

I came to Carthage, where a cauldron of illicit loves leapt and boiled about me. (3/1/1, p. 37)

T.S. Eliot puts this line into his own poetry, identifying himself and his whole civilization with Augustine:

> To Carthage then I came
> Burning burning burning burning
> O Lord Thou pluckest me out
> O Lord Thou pluckest
> burning

Carthage was very much like any great American city: New York, San Francisco, New Orleans, Cambridge, Massachusetts. It offered Augustine a fashionable moral relativism, unrestricted sex, media entertainment (theaters and gladiatorial contests), and a great variety of opportunities in higher education, especially in rhetoric, Augustine's chosen expertise, and in philosophy. It also offered a variety of religions, including heretical sects like Manicheeism that claimed to be Christian. Augustine tried them all, including what he thought he sampled in his first reading of the Bible, which he rejected as primitive and unsophisticated. But his restless heart found no rest.

I was not yet in love, but I was in love with love. . . . I sought some object to love, since I was thus in love

> **with loving. . . . For within I was hungry, all for the want of . . . Thyself, my God.** (3/1/1, p. 37)

Not in love (with a person) but in love with love—exactly the typically modern subjectivism that defines the difference between true love and lust. True love starts with vision: a vision of the beloved as a good person who deserves and/or needs my love. Lust starts with desire, with my own need for an object to elicit the pleasurable *experience* of love, which is the thing I crave. It is like the difference between appreciating a good wine—that particular unique one—and alcoholism, which is addiction not to a wine but to an experience.

It is idolatry, of course ("all for want of . . . Thyself, my God"), the sin against the first and foundational of all the commandments. We are created and designed to adore, and if we do not know its true object, we must adore false ones as our greatest good.

But it is not just that the sex partner is mistaken for God, but also that the experience of being "in love" is mistaken for the experience of Beatitude. What is lacking in the object of idolatrous love is God, of course; but what is lacking in the human subject, the idolater, is the *vision*. Christ confessed to His Father: "This is eternal life, that they know you" (Jn 17:3). Scripture calls sex between spouses a "knowing". (When Adam "knew" Eve, he did not write a psychology book but procreated a baby.) That personal knowing is what is missing in the darkness, fog, and confusion of lust. True love is the knowledge of a person; lust is the desire for a feeling.

> **O my God, my Mercy, with how much bitterness didst Thou in Thy goodness sprinkle the delights of**

> **that time! I was loved, and our love came to the bond of consummation: I wore my chains with bliss but with torment too, for I was scourged with the red hot rods of jealousy, with suspicions and fears and tempers and quarrels.** (3/1/1, p. 37)

Suffering, especially when it is brought on by our own follies, addictions, and idolatries, is "a severe mercy"—like the spurs used by the wise and loving rider to strike the horse's side with moderate pain to keep it on track. If God is love, then this *must* be the reason for suffering: that God wills our maximal joy, in the long run, and He sees that we need to suffer minimal pains, in the short run, in order to free us from the minimal joys which are our obstacles to our maximal joy.

Saint Teresa of Avila says that even if we have lived a life of horrible pains, when we look at these pains from the viewpoint of our Heavenly destiny, they will seem no more than "one night in an inconvenient hotel". That is not provable, but it is believable. It is logically possible, intellectually respectable. The fact that we are not God (have we digested this news yet?) and therefore do not share His providential omniscience and do not yet see how our pains help us does not refute the idea that God is love.

Of course lust gives us temporary joys, but its consequences, as Augustine discovers by experience here, are never joy or even settled happiness, but only temporary pleasures—and pains. Love's consequences are perfect and lasting joy, even in this life. The saints are the happiest people in the world. And this tells us something. For "you will know them by their fruits." (Mt 7:16).

Lust's consequences are verifiable very quickly. It is an

addiction, and therefore Augustine calls it "chains". Totally honest to all the data, Augustine confesses that he wore these chains with "bliss"; but for the same reason he confesses their "torment". Any addict, sexual or nonsexual, can verify this twofold psychological discovery. The only attachment that frees us is our attachment to God and to that which God is: truth and love. All others enslave and constrict us like a boa constrictor. This constitutes experiential verification for the rightness of God's first and greatest commandment. Those who worship what is less than themselves (including their own experience) become less than themselves. Those who worship the One who is more than themselves become more than themselves.

Critique of the Theater

I developed a passion for stage plays, with the mirror they held up to my own miseries and the fuel they poured on my flame. (3/2/2, p. 37)

Children objectify and distance themselves from real dangers by playing games about them (war, cops and robbers, pirates, etc.). We, too, distance ourselves from life's tragedies by objectifying them in theatrical performances. The principle is similar to inoculation, i.e., injecting a mild dosage of a disease (e.g., cowpox) into our bloodstream to stimulate the body to produce antigens to protect it from the more serious disease (e.g., smallpox). But the feelings we evoke in the theater are not "the real thing", they are just surface feelings, not whole-person doings. We just sit passively and weep, and we enjoy our weeping; we do not go out of ourselves in charity to aid the sufferers. That will be Augustine's critique of the theater in the next quotation.

This is a very up-to-date issue, since "media" are even more powerful in our culture than in Augustine's. It does not matter much whether the plays are on a live stage, a movie screen, or a computer screen. Their psychological role is the same, whatever their degree of technological sophistication.

How is it that a man wants to be made sad by the sight of tragic sufferings that he could not bear in

> **his own person? Yet the spectator does want to feel sorrow, and it is actually his feeling of sorrow that he enjoys.** (3/2/2, pp. 37–38)

A soap opera will not be successful unless it gives us "a good cry". Our most popular literary productions are tragedies, not comedies. Augustine's nose for mystery sniffs one out here: Why do we enjoy contemplating sufferings on stage that we do not enjoy contemplating in real life, either when we feel them in ourselves or when we see them in our friends? Why do we actually enjoy our very feeling of sorrow that we experience when we watch them on stage? How can sorrows be joys?

The answer will be twofold. First, as explained above, we are only playing. That is why we call them "plays". We pull the teeth of these fearful lions by turning them into fictions, as explained above. And there is nothing wrong with that; in fact it is wise. We are rehearsing, preparing to deal with real lions (tragedies) if we should meet them off the stage. But the second answer is not so wise:

> **Now when a man suffers himself, it is called misery; when he suffers in the suffering of another, it is called pity. But how can the unreal sufferings of the stage possibly move pity? The spectator is not moved to aid the sufferer but merely to be sorry for him. . . . That is why I loved those sorrows—not that I wanted them to bite too deep (for I had no wish to suffer the sorrows I loved to look upon), but simply to scratch the surface of my heart as I saw them on the stage.** (3/2/2, 4, pp. 38–39)

When we see another person suffer, we are in a dilemma. Either we relieve the sufferings or we do not. If we do, that must be by bearing some of his burdens ourselves, either physically or emotionally, by empathy. And that is painful. But if we do not relieve the sufferings, we feel the moral pain of guilt. The theater allows us to *feel* passively very moral without actually being moral in action. It is a substitute for sacrifice.

We love to praise virtues we already have and denounce vices of which we are rarely guilty. But we hate to hear critiques of vices to which we are addicted and calls for virtues we have never practiced. How often do we hear homilies denouncing cold-heartedness and encouraging "compassion"? How many do we hear denouncing lust and exhorting us to chastity? Do a word count.

> **Is compassion, feeling for others, therefore to be shunned? By no means. The sorrows of others must move our love.** (3/2/3, p. 38)

A bad thing is always the corruption of a good thing. Compassion, even in the merely emotional sense of the word, is a good thing, in fact a very good thing, because it moves us to something greater than itself, namely, active love, charity. But to let the feeling substitute for the doing is not a good thing. Good feelings can no more do the work of good deeds than they can do the work of good thoughts. God gave us hearts, hands, and heads, and no one of them can do the work of any of the others.

The Conversion to Philosophy

> **Following the normal order of study I had come to a book of one Cicero, whose tongue practically everyone admires, though not his heart. That particular book is called *Hortensius* and contains an exhortation to philosophy. Quite definitely it changed the direction of my mind, altered my prayers to You, O Lord, and gave me a new purpose and ambition. Suddenly all the vanity I had hoped in I saw as worthless, and with an incredible intensity of desire I longed after immortal wisdom. I had begun that journey upwards by which I was to return to You. . . . For with You is wisdom. Now love of wisdom is what is meant by the Greek word "philosophy", and it was to philosophy that that book set me so ardently.** (3/4/7–8, pp. 40–41)

Here is what we may call Augustine's "first conversion", or the first part of his conversion. Though it was a book of philosophy that occasioned it, it was a conversion not merely of Augustine's mind but of his heart. He fell in love with a divine attribute, wisdom; he discovered his first absolute.

Notice how different Augustine's and Cicero's and Socrates' notion (and practice!) of philosophy is from that of most philosophers today. The technical analysis of language, the cultivation of cleverness, and the idolatry of scholarship are not yet "the love of wisdom"; they just stole the name.

Only later in his life did Augustine recognize the source of what happened to him when he read Cicero's book. It was the presence and activity of God in him, the God he did not know at the time as the God of Christianity. But God is not proud: He often operates anonymously.

Cicero's book has been lost to history. Its effect on its most famous reader has not.

Augustine, more than any other individual, created the mind of the Middle Ages and, thereby, also the modern Western civilization that rested on it. If Augustine had never discovered Cicero, who largely made it possible for him to discover Christ, the whole history of the Western world would have been radically changed.

> **But the one thing that delighted me in Cicero's exhortation was that I should love, and seek, and win, and hold, and embrace, not this or that philosophical school but Wisdom itself, whatever it might be.** (3/4/8, p. 41)

War, politics, sports, family loyalty, religion—all these are by nature divisive, partisan, either/or. Philosophy is usually the same: "my" philosophy vs. yours, Platonism vs. Aristotelianism. Ideologies are divisive. But philosophy is not an ideology. Augustine, like Socrates, sees philosophy as the love of "Wisdom itself, whatever it might be". No matter how great a philosopher Plato is, Platonism is not an absolute or a universal good; wisdom is. Wisdom is to the soul what food is to the body; how absurd it would be if we were divided by food ideologies: beef-ism vs. lamb-ism, fruit-ism vs. vegetable-ism.

It is significant that Christianity was never called "Christianism". Christianity is not an ideology. Christ is the human Incarnation of the divine Logos, the divine Mind, the divine Wisdom, and as such is the universal "light that enlightens every man who comes into the world" (Jn 1:9). As Arthur Holmes put it, "all truth is God's truth."

> **The book excited and inflamed me; in my ardour the only thing I found lacking was that the name of Christ was not there. For with my mother's milk my infant heart had drunk in, and still held deep down in it, that name . . . ; and whatever lacked that name, no matter how learned and excellently written and true, could not win me wholly.** (3/4/8, p. 41)

Augustine thinks deeply about memory in book 10 and about how it enriches life by because the *Confessions* is itself a long memory. Memory is a joining of the present and the past, and the *Confessions* is a joining of the mature, Christian mind *with which* Augustine is remembering and the immature, pre-Christian mind *that* he is remembering. He could not have written this statement about Christ when he first read Cicero, at nineteen, for he literally didn't know what he was missing in reading Cicero, because he did not yet know Christ. But the name of Christ was in fact missing, and that is why even Cicero did not still his restless heart.

Yet in another sense Christ was not missing but present. For it was Christ Who not only led Augustine providentially to Cicero but also inspired his falling in love with Wisdom through Cicero. That was Christ really present, but it was Christ anonymously present. That is precious, but it is not sufficient. The heart does not rest until it sees its anonymous lover face to face. That is why even our most mature and best knowledge of Christ in this life is not sufficient. "A man's reach should exceed his grasp, Or what's a heaven for?" (Robert Browning).

When Augustine says that as an infant he had drunk in

the name of Christ with his mother's milk, this is not a mere image, a poetic juxtaposition; it is a real causal relation. The connection between a loving, praying mother and her loved, prayed-for, straying son is not merely physical ("milk") and not merely spiritual (prayer), but it is both at once. Breast milk is a prayer. It is love incarnate.

And it is not just a connection of efficient causality, or power; it is also a connection of formal causality, or identity. It is like a brand on cattle. For there is a spiritual as well as a physical dimension to heredity, since we are not merely physical creatures, as in modern materialism, or merely spiritual creatures, as in Gnosticism, or merely dualistic creatures, as in Cartesianism. We are neither animals nor angels nor animals *plus* angels. We are through and through hylomorphic or psychosomatic. That is why there is a "theology of the body". And we habitually forget this. That is why we are surprised by John Paul II's title when we first hear it. And that is also why we are surprised when Augustine says that he drank in the name of Christ as an infant with his mother's milk. A Cartesian would call that a "category confusion". But God Himself was responsible for that "category confusion" when He breathed into our body the Spirit of life (Gen 2:7).

When he deals with philosophical rather than religious issues, Augustine sometimes veers close to Platonic dualism —as when he interprets sensation as an act of "vital attention" of the soul alone, which conjures up a sense image in the physical organ; or when he defines man as "a soul using a body" (though he clearly affirms that the body is as essential to man's identity and definition as the soul). But his imagery, which comes unconsciously from his Christian faith, is often wiser than his philosophical concepts, which come consciously from his natural reason.

The Bible versus Manicheeism

So I resolved to make some study of the Sacred Scriptures and find what kind of books they were. But what I came upon was something not grasped by the proud, not revealed either to children, something utterly humble in the hearing but sublime in the doing, and shrouded deep in mystery. And I was not of the nature to enter into it or bend my neck to follow it. When I first read those Scriptures, I did not feel in the least what I have just said; they seemed to me unworthy to be compared with the majesty of Cicero. My conceit was repelled by their simplicity, and I had not the mind to penetrate into their depths. (3/5/9, pp. 41–42)

One way the Bible is unique is that it combines profound and inexhaustible depths, which no theologian or even mystic can exhaust, with a simple, clear, and obvious surface meaning that even a child can grasp. But the only way into its adult depths is a childlike (but not childish) acceptance of its surface meaning by having the humility and the heart of a child. At this point in his life, Augustine had not yet grown up enough to become a child.

We can see the same three stages of growth here if we look at another issue. Imagine a father telling his young son not to visit internet porn sites or to experiment with drugs or to get drunk. As a prepubescent child, he does not understand the reason but humbly trusts his father and obeys.

Later, as a teenager, he becomes proud and arrogant and rebels, thinking he is wiser than his father and wiser than he used to be as a child, when in fact he is more foolish. Still later, as a mature adult child, he understands his father's wisdom: the harm to himself in cultivating an addiction. Again he trusts and obeys, but now more freely and maturely, from the wisdom of sad experience. (It is fools who learn by experience.) Now he understands his father. Mark Twain said: "When I was a boy of fourteen, my father was so ignorant I could hardly stand to have the old man around. But when I got to be twenty-one, I was astonished at how much the old man had learned in seven years."

What applies to the earthly father also applies to the Heavenly Father and to His Word. We typically move through these three phases regarding many things in life. One of these things is understanding the Bible. Once again Augustine is typical, and typically modern.

> **I fell in with a sect of men** [the Manichees] **talking high-sounding nonsense. . . .** [T]**he names of God the Father and of the Lord Jesus Christ and of the Paraclete, the Holy Ghost, our Comforter . . . were always on their lips, but only as sounds and tongue noises; for their heart was empty of the true meaning. They cried out "Truth, truth;" they were forever uttering the word to me, but the thing was nowhere in them. . . . O Truth, Truth, how inwardly did the very marrow of my soul pant for You when time and again I heard them sound Your name. But it was all words.** (3/6/10, p. 42)

> **I swallowed them because I thought that they were Yourself; yet I did not swallow them with much ap-**

> **petite, because You did not taste in my mouth as You are—for after all You were not those empty falsehoods—and I was not nourished by them, but utterly dried up. Food in dreams is exactly like real food, yet what we eat in our dreams does not nourish: for we are dreaming.** (3/6/10, p. 43)

Manicheeism was to Catholic Christianity what Starbucks coffee is to Dunkin Donuts coffee: the new, expensive, complex, revised version for sophisticates. (Starbucks lovers, please forgive my populist prejudice!)

Augustine's criticism does not go into the details here of the contradictions between the Manichean version of Christianity and what both the Church and the Bible taught—e.g., that there were two Gods, not one; that the good God did not create matter; and that matter, not personal sin, was the cause of evil. Instead, he focuses on the very last thing a typically modern critic would think of: it wasn't *true*. It was just words. And since it wasn't true, it didn't satisfy the truth-seeking depths of Augustine's heart ("the very marrow of my soul"). A placebo can "cure" an imaginary disease, but only a real medicine and a real doctor can cure a real one. Dreams can only change other dreams; they can't change reality.

"Truth", for Augustine, means not merely the correctness of an idea (and certainly not the social acceptability of an idea or the "political correctness" of an ideology) but something that inheres in reality, not just ideas: "the real thing", authenticity. Truth is not just epistemological but ontological. It is the opposite of the *fake*.

We all have an innate truth-detector. It is, of course, fallible, like everything human; but it is really there. And Augustine's truth-detector is unusually sensitive, both to truth and to error. For it is very critical and demanding and questioning: look at all those interrogative sentences in the *Confessions*. It could not be satisfied with clever fakes like Manicheeism for very long (actually, it was eleven years), while Christ satisfied it forever.

> **How far then is the reality of You from** [1] **those empty imaginings of mine, imaginings of bodies which had no being whatever.** [2] **The images of those bodies which do have being are more certain than they, and** [3] **the bodies themselves more certain than the images. Yet even these You are not. You are not even** [4] **the soul, which is the life of bodies—and therefore obviously better and more certain than the bodies it vivifies: but You are** [5] **the Life of souls, the Life of lives, Livingness itself, and You shall not change, O Life of my soul.** (3/6/10, p. 43)

I inserted the numbers to distinguish the five levels of reality Augustine distinguishes here. God (5) gives life to souls (4); souls (4) give life to bodies (3); bodies (3) give life to true sense images of them (2); and the "empty imaginings" of Manicheeism (1) are not even as real as real images (2), since they do not come from objective reality at all.

Augustine classifies Manicheeism as "empty imaginings" (1) because it was a false truth-claim about bodies (3) as well as about souls (4) and about God (5), just as Christianity is a true truth-claim about bodies (ours and Christ's) as well as about souls and about God.

Augustine will later repeat the point about God being "the [supernatural, eternal] Life of souls" as souls are the (natural, temporal) life of bodies. His point is not that God and the human soul make one being, as our soul and our body make one being, but that our soul is as dependent on God as our body is dependent on our soul. God is not just an addition to our souls but the very life of our souls, at every minute, as our souls are the very life of our bodies. Without Him, our souls lack not just truth, goodness, and joy but also life itself, existence itself, both natural and supernatural. Our souls "breathe" Him.

The Three Big Problems

Next, Augustine lists the three main philosophical and theological problems he could not solve, his three main intellectual obstacles to Christianity: the problem of evil (if God is all-good, how can there be evil?), the problem of God (how is He imaginable?), and the problem of morality (is it relative and changing or not?).

> **But I did not know that other reality which truly is; and through my own sharpness I let myself be taken in by fools, who deceived me with such questions as:**
>
> [1] **Whence comes evil?**
>
> [2] **And is God bounded by a bodily shape and has he hair and nails?**
>
> [3] **And are those** [patriarchs] **to be esteemed righteous who had many wives at the same time and slew men and offered sacrifices of living animals?** (3/7/12, p. 44)

He then very briefly lists the answers he would later find to the first two questions and spends considerable time making important distinctions concerning the third one:

> [1] **I did not know that evil has no being of its own but is only an absence of good.** (3/7/12, p. 44)
>
> [2] **I did not even know that God is a spirit, having no parts extended in length and breadth, to whose being**

> **bulk does not belong, for bulk is less in its part than in the whole . . . and so could not be wholly itself in every place, as a spirit is, as God is.** (3/7/12, p. 44)
>
> [3] **Nor did I know that true and inward righteousness which judges not according to custom but according to the most righteous law of Almighty God. By that law the ways of conduct of different places and times are shaped as is best for those places and times, though the law itself is always and everywhere the same, not different in different places or changing with the ages. . . . [I]n the one dwelling house and the one family the same things are not allowed to every member of the household and in all parts of the house. . . . Does this mean that justice is unstable and changeable? No, but the times over which justice presides are not alike, for they are times.** (3/7/13, p. 45)

This third question is the main problem our own culture has with Christianity. It is the apparent truth of moral relativism.

To distinguish the relative and changing from the absolute and unchanging, one must clearly grasp the absolute and unchanging, for it is the touchstone and standard. At this time in his life, Augustine could not do that. It is as if he could not see the unmoving hinge of the arm of a pendulum, but only the swinging, moving ball and arm. The ball symbolizes human situations that change in time, in the course of the history of an individual and of the race. The hinge symbolizes absolute and unchanging goods or values, which are based on the very nature of God. The arm symbolizes the law or will of God. God wills somewhat different things for different times and situations precisely because of the unchanging and universal values (love, justice, truth, salvation) that are often realized differently in different particular times and places and situations.

For instance, take justice. Until they come of age, It is just for children to be driven but not to drive; later, it is just for them to drive and not always to be driven. Same justice, different applications. The arm of the pendulum (the law) must often change to follow the changing ball at its lower end (the situation) precisely out of fidelity to the unchanging hinge at its upper end (the eternal values). Another example: democracy is a just political regime for a relatively mature and educated people but not for a primitive and uneducated one. Another: the same justice that demands that mature siblings have essentially equal authority with each other in collective decision making also demands that young children do *not* have equal authority with their parents.

But sometimes not only the values, or principles, but also the concrete applications of values are also unchangingly bad or good. Some acts are never wrong (e.g., to love God), and some are never right (e.g., sodomy). It is significant that the one act that Augustine selects as the most obvious of all examples of an evil act is one that every public society in the entire history of the world has agreed is unnatural—except our own. Does that tell against Augustine and all mankind or against us?

In no time or place could it be wrong for a man to love God with his whole heart and his whole soul and his whole mind, and his neighbour as himself. Therefore those sins which are against nature, like those of the men of Sodom, are in all times and places to

> **be detested and punished. Even if all nations committed such sins, they should all alike be held guilty by God's law which did not make men so that they should use each other thus.** (3/8/15, p. 46)

If even this (one of the six "sins that cry to Heaven for vengeance", according to the traditional list) is not intrinsically evil, Augustine implies, then nothing is. A universal moral relativism is the logical consequence of denying such obvious-until-now examples as this—or (an even more obvious and deadly example) the deliberate murder by a mother of her own child in her womb. The fact that sins are widely practiced does not make them innocent. When poisons become popular, they do not become less deadly, but more.

Our whole civilization is now living in the moral confusion through which Augustine lived. Will we come out of it, as he did? That probably depends on how many Monicas we have.

> **Actions which are against the customs of human societies are to be avoided according to the variety of such customs. . . . But when God orders something against the custom or covenant of a state, though it never had been done it must be done.** (3/8/15, p. 46)

Human laws, customs, and traditions have a human authority, which is real but not absolute; but God has the absolute authority to override them. Thus only religion justifies social rebellion. The judge must transcend the judged.

Conventional wisdom contrasts secular "radicals" with religious "conservatives". This is upside down. For only if one believes, as "conservatives" do, in unchanging absolutes can one have moral justification for a radical critique of one's society, like the prophets of ancient Israel. If there is no higher law than human law, then one must logically be a stick-in-the-mud conservative. Logically, atheists must worship the State, or, in a democracy, "consensus", for there is nothing higher. If religion dies, politics takes its place.

> **Thus many actions that to men seem blameworthy, are approved in Your sight; and many that are praised by men are condemned by You, O God—all because often the appearance of the act may be quite different from the mind of the doer or because there is some unrealised element in the situation.** (3/9/17, p. 48)

Augustine here lists the three factors, or dimensions, of a freely chosen human act that make it morally good or evil in the eyes of God and therefore in reality:

(1) the act itself, as it appears in the world,
(2) the mind and motive of the doer, and
(3) the situation or circumstances.

Only if all three line up, only if all three are right, is the act good. We must (1) do the right thing, (2) for the right reason, (3) in the right way and in the right situation.

The first is objective and universal (or unchanging): always do the right thing.

The second is subjective and universal: always have the right motive.

The third is objective and particular: do what is truly needed for the situation.

Legalism ("just obey the law") is satisfied with (1) alone.

Subjectivism ("just be sincere" or "just be compassionate") is satisfied with (2) alone.

Pragmatism or utilitarianism ("do what works") is satisfied with (3) alone.

God is satisfied only when all the dimensions are right, just as we are satisfied with a novel or a play only when all its dimensions are good: plot, characters, setting, style, and theme; and just as we are satisfied only if all the organs in our body are healthy and working properly, not just one or two.

Monica's Tears

And You *sent Your hand from above*, and *raised my soul out of* that depth of darkness because my mother, Your faithful one, wept to You for me more bitterly than mothers weep for the bodily deaths of their children. (3/11/19, p. 49)

If you asked Augustine what caused his conversion, his first answer would be: Monica's love and prayers. Prayer really changes things. Hers changed the history of Western civilization.

Trying to do great good in this world without prayer is like trying to win a war without any air force. That supernatural air force is really there (unless religion is the world's biggest lie) and ready to fight, but it waits for our signals. Those signals are faith, hope, and, above all, passionate charity. All three are proved by prayer.

You gave her another assurance by the mouth of Your priest, a certain bishop reared up in the Church and well grounded in Your Scriptures. My mother asked him in his kindness to have some discussion with me, to refute my errors, to unteach me what was evil and teach me what was good, for he often did this when he found such people as it might profit. He refused, rightly as I have realised since. He told her that I was

> **as yet not ripe for teaching because I was all puffed up with the newness of my heresy. . . .**
>
> **When he had told her this, my mother would not be satisfied but urged him with repeated entreaties and floods of tears to see me and discuss with me. He, losing patience, said: "Go your way; as sure as you live, it is impossible that the son of these tears should perish." In the conversations we had afterwards, she often said that she had accepted this answer as if it had sounded from heaven.** (3/12/21, pp. 50–51)

The priest and bishop was Ambrose. Like Augustine and Monica, he was to become a canonized saint, though none of the three involved in this holy triangle had any idea of that future.

Monica demanded that Ambrose, who indeed had the answers, give them to Augustine ("refute my errors") right away. She had the persistence of a Jewish mother and would not take No for an answer. But Ambrose was the better psychologist and realized that sick souls, like sick bodies, need patient care, not instant fixing like broken machines. Ambrose was more patient here with the heretic (Augustine) than with the saint (Monica).

But God used Ambrose's very fault of "losing patience" with Monica to satisfy Monica. When Augustine says that "she had accepted this answer ('It is impossible that the son of these tears should perish') as if it had sounded from heaven", he does not mean to imply by this "as if" that it did not really come from Heaven, but just the opposite: that it did. Monica accepted this answer, not on Ambrose's authority, but on God's. For as Elihu says to Job, "God speaks in one way, and in two, though man does not perceive it" (Job 33:14).

When Henry Coray wrote a novel about Augustine, he entitled it *Son of Tears*. (It's worth reading. The Augustine movie *Restless Heart* is better.) Tears are like blood: they come from a broken heart. They are also water: they produce new life. If they proceed from faith, hope, and charity, they are participations in the blood and water that poured from Christ's pierced heart on the Cross.

Astrology

> [Astrologers] **teach that the inevitable cause of sin is in the heavens, that it is the doing of Venus or Saturn or Mars: in other words that man, flesh and blood and proud corruption, is guiltless, and that the guilt lies with the Creator and Ruler of heaven and the stars of heaven.** (4/3/4, p. 57)

Carthage was very much like any modern American city, and Augustine found and worshipped many of the same idols there as we find and worship here (sex, entertainment, education, ideology, false religion). Not only was the great question the same (what gives human life its meaning and purpose?), but the great answers were also the same. Astrology was one of them.

Simple, literal astrology is not as popular today as it was in Augustine's time, but three far more sophisticated and supposedly scientific versions of it are Darwinism, Marxism, and Freudianism. All give mankind exactly the same supposed benefit or payoff as astrology: exculpation from guilt. The practical bottom line of all three modern theories is the same as that of astrological fatalism: that "man, flesh and blood and proud corruption, is guiltless." Darwinians tell us that we ape the apes, not because we are wicked, but because we are their children, not God's. Marxists tell us that there is no personal sin, only economic sin; that our faults are the faults of our capitalist system. Freudians tell us that we are an id, not an ego; an *it*, not an *I*; a river of libido, not a person who has the reason and free will to control his boat on this river. Astrology still rules; the only difference is that the stars have fallen to earth.

A Traumatic Death

> [A] **very dear friend . . . died. And I was not there. My heart was black with grief. Whatever I looked upon had the air of death. My native place was a prison house and my home a strange unhappiness. The things we had done together became sheer torment without him. My eyes were restless looking for him, but he was not there. I hated all places because he was not in them. They could not say "He will come soon," as they would in his life when he was absent.** (4/4/7–9, pp. 58–59)

Death is always traumatic, but much more so when the victim is young, when the death is sudden, when the bereaved feels guilty for not having been there, and especially when the bereaved does not yet know the true God, Who conquered death.

Augustine keenly observes a surprising phenomenon in himself, one that many of the bereaved have observed: Although the victim was only a small part of Augustine's world, it seemed as if his whole world had died: "*Whatever* I looked upon had the air of death." As C. S. Lewis put it, in *A Grief Observed*, when his wife died, "her absence was like the sky, spread over everything."

Why? How can one small person leave a universe-sized hole?

Because your friend is a part of yourself.

The only thing that is a part of every experience you ever have is yourself. (God is also present in every experience, but Augustine did not know the true God yet.) The instruments through which you know physical things are your physical eyes and the instruments that magnify them, like telescopes. But the instrument through which you know other people is your self, your soul. That is why, when that instrument changes, everything changes.

And that instrument changed when Augustine's friend died because his friend was not just a part of his world, an object; he was also part of Augustine's self, he was a co-subject. He was not an "it" but a "you", who, together with Augustine's "I", made a "we"; and that "we" now no more existed.

Here is a concrete image for this abstract point. When one of the two lenses in your eyeglasses cracks, the whole world looks like a cracked world. Your friend and you were like two lenses, standing together side by side looking at the same world. You had two sets of eyes. In fact you had two sets of *I*'s, two souls as well as two bodies. Thus, even the sober and unpoetical Aristotle said that "a friend is another self", or "the other half of your soul", your other eye. When he was alive, your friendship gave you a sense of depth and perspective: you looked at the world with two sets of eyes. Now that he is dead, you are a Cyclops, a one-eyed creature. You see the same world, but without the other dimension.

To see that this is a fact, not just an image, just cover up one eye for a while.

I became a great enigma to myself and I was forever asking my soul why it was sad and why it disquieted me so sorely. And my soul knew not what to

> **answer me. If I said *Trust in God*, my soul did not obey—naturally, because the man whom she had loved and lost was nobler and more real than the imagined deity in whom I was bidding her trust.** (4/4/9, pp. 59–60)

> **For my God was not yet You but the error and vain fantasy I held. When I tried to rest my burden upon that, it fell as through emptiness and was once more heavy upon me.** (4/7/12, p. 62)

Augustine is constantly having a dialogue with himself. When he is unquiet of heart, he is also unquiet about *why* he is unquiet. Neither heart nor head ever shut down.

At the time of his friend's death, he is not yet a Christian, but he is not an atheist either, so he tries religious faith ("trust in God"). But it does not work, because its object is not the real God but a mere idea. And a mere idea, even an idea of an immortal and omnipotent Supreme Being, is less real than an objectively real mortal. Trying to rest his grief on that was like trying to rest a cannonball on a cloud.

We see again that Augustine's fundamental drive is an ontological thirst, a thirst for *being*, for reality. What is the test for the difference between mere subjective ideas and objective realities? How can we tell whether something (in this case Augustine's "God" at that time) is a mere idea or an objective reality? It is really very simple: mere ideas, by themselves, can change only other ideas; they cannot change reality. But realities can change both other realities and our ideas.

That is why Saint Paul prays for his bereaved readers, "that you may not grieve as others do who have no hope" (1 Thess 4:13). God can raise both the dead in the world and hope in the soul; our own minds can do neither.

> **I had no delight but in tears, for tears had taken the place my friend had held in the love of my heart.** (4/4/9, p. 60)

How can tears of *sorrow* be *comforting* when a friend dies? Because they are friend-shaped tears. They are like memories or photographs of him that are so vivid that they are almost alive.

That is why it is not an act of kindness or comfort to say to the bereaved, "Don't weep." Tell them to weep. Weep with them. That is what Jesus did (Jn 11:35). That shortest verse in the Bible is also one of the most comforting.

Your with-ness with the bereaved can be a little substitute, however inadequate, for his with-ness with the friend he has lost. In other words, your presence is the same kind of comfort as his tears. Especially if you add your tears to his. (Remember that great scene in the attic in *Shadowlands*!)

> **I was at once utterly weary of life and in great fear of death.** (4/6/11, p. 61)

This is a terrible dilemma because life and death are the only two alternatives. It's like the line from "Old Man River": "I'm tired of livin' and scared of dyin'."

> **It may be that the more I loved him the more I hated and feared, as the cruellest enemy, that death which had taken him from me; and I was filled with the thought that it might snatch away any man as suddenly as it had snatched him.** (4/6/11, p. 61)

Pop psychology teaches us to "accept" death as "another stage of growth"; and Freud tells us we must "make friends with the necessity of dying". But to anyone who loves life, this is treason. Simply to "accept" anyone's death is proof that your love is weak. The more you love a person, the more you hate the death that is his enemy. Thus Dylan Thomas says to his old, dying father: "Do not go gentle into that good night . . . ; rage, rage against the dying of the light."

And when someone close to you suddenly dies, you quickly realize your own vulnerability and how you had ignored it until now. In Tolstoy's masterpiece *The Death of Ivan Ilyich*, Ivan had long known, from a logic class, that "all men are mortal." But this was an abstract, impersonal fact about man in general. Only when he contracted a fatal disease did he truly "know" death. It was a wholly different kind of knowledge. Augustine is coming a little closer to that deeper knowledge here.

And that will speed his conversion. Death is a great motivator. There are few sins or follies we will commit on our deathbed. That is why it is good to realize that our deathbed began when we were born.

> **I wondered that other mortals should live when he was dead whom I had loved as if he would never die. . . .** (4/6/11, p. 61) **O madness that knows not how to love men as men!** (4/7/12, p. 61)

Imagine the shock if you knew that the God you worshipped had died forever. That is the shock all idolaters get, for all idols die. That is true even of what is perhaps the very best of all idols, our beloved friends. To love anything as if it would never die is to love it as if it were God. And that is idolatry. And the best idols are the worst, the most dangerous. No one goes to Hell for idolizing paper clips. But many Pharisees went to Hell for worshipping their religion instead of God.

That does not mean we should be such prudent, rational Stoics; that we do not give our hearts to any human being, lest they be broken. That kind of "rationality" is the very definition of Hell. Love is not "rational"; love is crazy, but love is the only way to Heaven. The only Heavenly heart is a broken heart. The heart of Jesus was broken; how dare we think we do not need to be conformed to His image?

Love is not Stoically "rational", but it is not irrational either. Everything must be loved as it is: God as God, men as men, things as things. God must be loved with adoration, with the whole heart. Others must be loved with charity and goodwill, as we love ourselves (because they *are* the other half of the self, or at least equal to the self), but not with adoration, as God must be loved. And things, unlike divine or human persons, must be loved not as ends, but as means, with proper use and real but limited appreciation.

> [A]**nd I marvelled still more that he should be dead and I his other self living still. Rightly has a friend been called "the half of my soul." For I thought of my soul and his soul as one soul in two bodies; and my life was a horror to me because I would not live halved.** (4/6/11, p. 61)

Why are corpses and ghosts the two staples of most horror movies? No one has ever been physically harmed by either one. Because they are the two halves of a human being without the other: corpses are bodies without souls, and ghosts are souls without bodies. If a friend is "the half of my soul", as Aristotle said, then life without that half is a horror for the same reason a ghost or a corpse is a horror.

"I would not live *halved*." The top half of a body without the bottom would be a horror. So is the bottom half without the top. A soul with a mind but no heart would be a horror. So is a soul with a heart but no mind. Similarly, a soul without a body or a body without a soul is a horror. And one friend without the other, one in the world of the living and one in the world of the dead, is the same kind of horror. It is profoundly *wrong*. We all sense that wrongness, instinctively. Bodies, souls, the body-soul unity, and a pair of friends all should not be cut in half. Death is horrible because it does that.

> **And it may be that I feared to die lest thereby he should die wholly whom I loved so deeply.** (4/6/11, p. 61)

Still another reason for grief. (Augustine is never satisfied!) If my friend is the other half of my soul, then I must die twice: once when that other half dies and once when I die. And since I am also half of his soul, he must also die twice, once when he dies and once when I do. Thus death is quadruply tragic: for the double loss of myself and for the double loss of my "other self". The previous reason for grief was apparently unselfish (because it mourned *his* death), but it was really also selfish (because it was also about half of *mine*); and this reason is apparently selfish (I feared my own death) but really also unselfish (because it feared the last half of *his* death). In the higher mathematics of love and friendship, 2 = 1 and 1 = 2.

> **I remained to myself a place of unhappiness, in which I could not abide, yet from which I could not depart. For where was my heart to flee for refuge from my heart? Whither was I to fly from myself?** (4/7/12, p. 62)

The only two persons you can never, ever escape, even for an instant, either in time or eternity, are yourself and God. How terrible when either one becomes unendurable! (This is why suicide never ever works. It is also why atheism never works.)

When your self becomes "a place . . . in which I could not abide, yet from which I could not depart", we have a little foretaste of Hell. The dilemma is impossible of solution without God, who solves both halves of the dilemma because when we let Him come into us, He makes it possible for us to depart from ourselves and abide in our new selves, which are in Him.

Beauty and Logic

> **Where are you going? . . . What goal are you making for, wandering around and about by ways so hard and laborious? Rest is not where you seek it. Seek what you seek, but it is not where you seek it. You seek happiness of life in the land of death, and it is not there.** (4/12/18, p. 65)

This short quotation is really a summary of the whole of the *Confessions*—and of human life. Augustine is talking to himself (as usual); his deeper, wiser self is questioning his acting self and asking the most obvious and important of all questions for us travelers in time: Quo vadis? Where are you going? What is your final end, your purpose, your hope, your goal, your home, your peace?

The thing he seeks is not just some timeless, abstract "value" merely to "know" intellectually as the solution to a philosophical puzzle. It is a concrete destination of his concrete life's journey, and he wants to "know" it by existential experience, as Adam "knew" Eve. He is not a philosopher pondering a puzzle; he is a dog in a crate on a train traveling in the wrong direction because he has lost his Owner's dog tag. He is not just ignorant, he is *lost*.

His heart will help him find his way home. When he says "seek what you seek but it is not where you seek it", he is saying that the seeking is not wrong, though the direction in which he is seeking is; that the restless heart is wise but the mind that supplies its road map is not. For the peace, the happiness, the joy that his heart (and yours) seeks cannot in fact be found anywhere but in the true God Who designed that heart.

For God is not an *option*, for "religious people" only, whoever they are. God is the only game in town. No alternative, no creature here "in the land of death" can give life, can give deep, real, secure, and lasting happiness, to our souls.

That is the first foundational fact, the "bad news"; and it can be verified by experience. We do not need faith, just reason and honesty, to know that.

The second fact is the "good news" that the true God, the God who really exists, not just in our faith but in objective reality, is our total happiness, joy, and peace. To know that "good news"—to "know" God as God—does require faith. Augustine is on the twisting road to God even while he is on the road away from God, because it is God who is teaching him, through his restless heart, how twisting and unsatisfying his life is.

The very worst thing that could possibly happen to our world is not nuclear war or mass starvation or ecological disaster or even a "hard totalitarianism" like *1984*, but a "soft totalitarianism" like *Brave New World*, a worldwide level of creature-comfort and satisfaction that would still the heart and its restlessness and make it almost impossible for anyone to find true rest in God because no one would seek Him. A worldwide Sweden would be a far greater victory for Hell than a worldwide Haiti.

"A fool is someone who learns by experience", but at least he learns, if only he is honest with experience. The bad news that honest experience teaches us is that nothing but God satisfies. This "bad news", discovered by the restless heart, is really the second best news in the world, because it drives us to the Good News. The restless heart is the second best, because it drives us to our rest.

> **But these things I did not at that time know, and I was in love with those lower beauties . . . and I said to my friends: "Do we love anything save what is beautiful? What then is . . . beauty? What is it that allures us and delights us in the things we love?"** (4/13/20, p. 66)

Augustine, like Plato in the *Symposium*, notes that beauty and love always go together, for some kind of beauty is always the object of love. So to understand what love is, we should understand what beauty is. And since love is the meaning of life and life's highest value, beauty is not just a peripheral "extra" but a central, fundamental question.

But it is a mystery. We all know it when we see it, but we find it very hard to define. (Augustine said the same thing about *time*: we all *know* what it is, yet we can't *say* what it is.)

> **I composed certain books *De Pulchro et Apto*—on the Beautiful and the Fitting—two books or three, I fancy; You know, O God, for I do not remember. I no longer have them. Somehow or other they have been lost.** (4/13/20, pp. 66–67)

Since love was the center of Augustine's life, beauty was also. Thus his very first book was, appropriately, about this precious, central, and mysterious thing. One would expect that he would treasure this book both for its subject matter and for it being his very first book. So it is quite amazing that he so casually and without any moaning informs us that this firstborn intellectual child of his mind has been totally lost. I think most modern readers bemoan this loss more than Augustine himself did. For Beauty is one of the major topics about which very few if any philosophers have ever written truly great books. Plato (the *Symposium*) and Plotinus (*On Beauty*)—and then the great wave peters out in the sand.

> **Man is a great deep, Lord. You number his very hairs and they are not lost in Your sight: but the hairs of his head are easier to number than his affections and the movements of his heart.** (4/14/22, pp. 67–68)

Beauty is a matter of the heart. Science can progress endlessly from triumph to triumph in exploring and mapping bodies, both those that belong to the universe and those that belong to persons; but only God can have a clear and accurate science of the heart.

Any philosopher who does not appreciate the fact that "man is a great deep" (and there are many such philosophers!) is simply not worth listening to when he talks about human things.

> **And what did it profit me that when I was barely twenty years old there came into my hands, and I read and understood, alone and unaided, the book of Aristotle's *Ten Categories*—a book I had longed for as for some great and divine work because the master who taught me rhetoric at Carthage, and others held learned, mouthed its name with such evident pride?** (4/16/28, p. 70)

From the mysteries of beauty to the clarities of logic, Augustine's mind embraces it all. The world's first logic textbook, so abstract as to be a challenge to most readers today just as in Augustine's day (as I know from my experience as a teacher) was a "cinch" for him. Note again how casual and unselfconscious he is, with neither pride nor false modesty.

> **Not only did this not profit me, it actually did me harm, in that I tried to understand You, my God, marvellous in Your simplicity and immutability, while imagining that whatsoever had being was to be found within these ten categories—as if You were a substance in which inhered Your own greatness of beauty, as they might inhere in a body. In fact Your greatness and Your beauty are Yourself, whereas a body is not large and beautiful merely by being a body, because it would still be a body even if it were less large and less beautiful.** (4/16/29, p. 71)

Some think that science and logic, which validly map everything finite, should be able to comprehend anything that is real, even the infinite God. Others deny this but cannot give any reason for it that is not thoughtless, lazy, and sentimental. Augustine explains this reason in logical detail that is (ironically) taken from the very book he mastered, Aristotle's *Categories*. In other words, he shows logically how logic itself confesses itself impotent regarding God's being.

Here is an unpacking of Augustine's logical point. Logic is the science of arguing, of proving. But an argument (e.g., "All men are mortal, and Socrates is a man, therefore Socrates is mortal") must begin with a proposition (e.g., "All men are mortal"), and a proposition must begin with a term (e.g., "men"). Aristotle's *Categories* is the foundation for logic by classifying all possible terms.

The most basic division of terms is into *substances* (beings that exist in themselves rather than in another—in other words, things rather than the attributes of things) and *accidents*, or attributes or properties, which exist only in substances, as the attributes of substances. "Accidents" include quantities, qualities, relations, actions, times, places, etc. Substances are expressed in grammar as nouns, accidents as verbs, adjectives, adverbs, prepositions, or conjunctions.

Accidents are accidental. A substance would still be itself if it changed its accidents. For example, I am the same person if I get old, bald, heavy, inactive, arrested, widowed, or rich. But this distinction between substance and accidents does not apply to God. For all God's attributes are essential rather than accidental. God is not just good, true, and beautiful. God is goodness; God is truth; God is beauty. They are not just abstract qualities inhering in Him, they are His very eternal essence. And therefore, unlike the attributes of any creature, they are as unchangeable as He is.

This is true even of being itself: God is not just *a* being; He does not just *have* being; He *is* being. He does not just happen to exist, He *is* His existence; His very essence is existence, to put it in later, Thomistic, terms. To put it into Augustine's terms, God is being itself because He is eternal and unchangeable; all other beings, even spiritual beings, are changeable at least in their accidents.

Most medieval philosophers considered Aristotle the all-time master of natural realities and Plato the master of supernatural realities. At the center of the most famous of all philosophical paintings, *The School of Athens* by Raphael, we see these two greatest non-Christian philosophers walking side by side; Aristotle is pointing down to the earth, while Plato is pointing up to the heavens. That is why Augustine preferred Plato to Aristotle.

> [Concerning natural science] **Surely a man is unhappy even if he knows all these things but does not know You; and that man is happy who knows You even though he knows nothing of them; and the man who knows both You and them is not the happier for them but only on account of You.** (5/4/7, pp. 78–79)

Augustine is implicitly saying here that the knowledge of God transcends arithmetic. For his three points are that (1) to know everything else but not God is profitless and non-happifying; and (2) to know God but nothing else is profitable and happifying; and (3) to know both God and everything else is not any more profitable or happifying than to know God alone. For to know God *is* to know everything, not because God is everything (that's pantheism) but because He is the designer of everything, the meaning of everything, and the origin and end of everything. All the secrets of Hamlet are in Shakespeare.

Augustine elsewhere says that we must choose between imperfect knowledge of perfect things and perfect knowledge of imperfect things. We can have perfect, or at least adequate, knowledge of this imperfect world, but not of the perfect God. And even Aristotle said that the least knowledge of the most perfect things is rightly prized far above the most perfect knowledge of imperfect things. We may not agree with this—until we are on our deathbed. Then, no one complains that he has thought too much about God and the ultimate meaning of life and too little about the sciences of creatures.

The essential difference between the medieval mind and the modern mind is right here. We spend most of our time and love and energy and perfection on science, which is the more perfect knowledge of less perfect things; while the medievals spent most of their time and love and energy on theology, which is the less perfect knowledge of the most perfect thing. The medieval mind was primitive in its science but profound in its theology. The modern mind is the reverse.

What is the cause of these different choices? I think it is because we moderns are subjectivists while premoderns were objectivists. We moderns prioritize perfect subjective human *knowledge* (science), even if it has only imperfect things as its real objects (nature), while the medievals prioritized the perfect objective reality (God), even if it could be known only with very imperfect subjective human knowledge. That is also why premodern philosophy begins with metaphysics while modern philosophy begins with epistemology. We moderns are like teenagers, thinking first about ourselves; the medievals were like preteen children, thinking first about objective reality. They asked: What is the perfect Being? We ask: How can we perfect ourselves? They asked, unselfconsciously, "What is there?" We ask, self-consciously, "Who am I?"

Augustine is the one great exception to this rule. He is quintessentially medieval *and* quintessentially modern.

Escape from Carthage— and Monica—to Rome

At Carthage the licence of the students is gross and beyond all measure. They break in impudently and like a pack of madmen play havoc with the order which the master has established for the good of his pupils. (5/8/14, p. 83)

The violent protests of left-wing student radicals did not begin in the 1960s. Augustine ran into them and wisely ran the other way. He neither joined the bullies nor used force against them; he just left. For he saw that that was not only the end of discipline and the end of education, it was also the end of justice (the very thing the students claimed they were demanding).

But You, *O my Hope and my Portion in the land of the living*, forced me to change countries for my soul's salvation: You pricked me with such goads at Carthage as drove me out of it, and You set before me certain attractions by which I might be drawn to Rome—in either case using men who loved this life of death, one set doing lunatic things, the other promising vain things: and to reform my ways You secretly used their perversity and my own. (5/8/14, pp. 83–84)

Here is an instance of Augustine's answer to the atheist's objection that evil refutes God. God allows evil men to do evil things not only to preserve human free will but also because He uses the very evils He allows for the sake of eventual greater goods. The violence of the students at Carthage, which drove Augustine away, and the temptations of worldly fame, riches, and pleasures at Rome, which drew him there, though both were evil, were both used by God as riders use spurs on horses: as goads to produce movement on a road. The road of Augustine's life was one that only God could foresee. "God writes straight with crooked lines."

> **Why I left the one country and went to the other, You knew, O God, but You did not tell either me or my mother. She indeed was in dreadful grief at my going and followed me right to the seacoast. There she clung to me passionately, determined that I should either go back home with her or take her to Rome with me, but I deceived her with the pretence that I had a friend whom I did not want to leave until he had sailed off with a fair wind. Thus I lied to my mother, and such a mother; and so got away from her.** (5/8/15, p. 84)

Here are some more "crooked lines" with which God wrote straight. God allowed Augustine's lying to his mother to escape her and sail to Rome because He had prepared something there that was needed for his conversion and could not be found in Carthage: the wise and holy Saint Ambrose, who would be the main instrument for Augustine's conversion. In this same "allowing", God also disciplined Monica's imprudent micromanaging of her son. Her end was right (Augustine's conversion), but her means were wrong (her own worried "helicoptering"); and God, in order to give her the end that both He and Monica desired, had to use other means. And of course neither Monica nor Augustine could see all this at the time, but only later. Our rearward vision ("Epimetheus") is always clearer than our forward vision ("Prometheus").

Examples like this enable us to trust that God knows exactly what He is doing when He allows *apparently* pointless evils into our lives. The apparent does not equal the real for us, only for God. ("Know thyself." Remember Saint Catherine's four-word summary of wisdom.)

> **But this also You have mercifully forgiven me, bringing me from the waters of that sea, filled as I was with execrable uncleanness, unto the water of Your grace; so that when I was washed clean, the floods that poured from my mother's eyes, the tears with which daily she watered the ground towards which she bent her face in prayer for me, should cease to flow.** (5/8/15, p. 84)

What riches lie in a single image! Water is the most common form of matter on the surface of the earth, but also one of the richest and most profound. Augustine's intuitive mind perceives the real unity and connections among no less than five meanings of this image in a single sentence:

(1) the literal salty water of the Mediterranean Sea;

(2) the "living water" of divine grace, divine life (*zoe*) that God was preparing to infuse into Augustine's soul in Rome at his conversion;

(3) the water of baptism, whose physical washing of the body both symbolizes and effects the spiritual washing of the soul from Original Sin;

(4) the flood waters of Monica's saltwater tears, which were the powerful prayers that brought about Augustine's conversion (for remember, the tears *were* prayers; they were sacramental; they were not just the purely material *expressions* of her purely spiritual prayers); and

(5) the rain water from the heavens by which the earth is irrigated and which is the food of all plant life.

How does Augustine come by such depth of intuition into a many-layered symbol? This habit of mind, this intuition of connections and analogies, is a gift of God, who created and designed our minds. But it can be cultivated. It cannot be directly taught, like mathematics, but it can be "caught", like measles. It can be a good infection, and it is "caught" by exposure to and imitation of geniuses like Augustine who have already been "infected" by it.

> **That night I stole away without her: she remained praying and weeping. And what was she praying for, O my God, with all those tears but that You should not allow me to sail! But You saw deeper and granted the essential of her prayer: You did not do what she was at that moment asking, that You might do the thing she was always asking.** (5/8/15, p. 84)

Christ promises us that He will give us everything we ask for (Mk 11:24). Yet we often pray for things and they do not happen. Is there a catch, a gimmick, a trick? Not at all. The following explanation is not a "catch" at all, and as soon as we see the three simple points below, our minds easily understand and accept them, though our emotions usually can't keep up with our minds while we are hurting and worrying like Monica. That's OK: He promised real-good, not feel-good. Which would you prefer? We know more than we feel; would you really prefer that we didn't?

In the first place, He is obviously speaking about good things in His promises, not evil things. And we are often mistaken about what things are really good for us and even more often mistaken about what things are best for us.

But even so, many things that both God and we *know* are truly good and in accordance with His loving will, like a conversion or a recovery from a terrible illness, do not come to us, even when we pray for them. That is because, in the second place, everything in time takes time. God is a lover, not a train. He does not arrive on our timetables. He promises us everything good, but temporal goods take time. Not all things are immediately good, but "all things *work together for* good" (Rom 8:28, KJV).

In the third place—and this is the point on which Augustine focuses in the quotation above—God always gives us the good things we most deeply want, as He gave to Monica what Augustine called "the essential of her prayer", but not always what we think we want and consciously pray for. God is a great psychologist and understands our own subconscious depths perfectly. Often, the best way for us to get what we most deeply want is not to get what we consciously want. God often gives us our most deeply desired end precisely by denying us our asked-for means, or gives us our long-range ends by denying us our short-range means, because He sees clearly, as we do not, the whole providential picture and how best to work out *all* things for our *really best* good, while we can only ask for *some* things for our *apparent and immediate* good.

Once we get that greater good, in the end, we look back, with our Epimethean vision, and see how it was indeed best, and then we are grateful that He did not answer our shallower prayer. Sometimes we see this even in this life (as Monica did when Augustine was finally converted, in the famous scene in the garden). But most often we have to wait for the end before we see it—and this life is not the end.

> **The wind blew and filled our sails and the shore dropped from our sight. And the next morning she was frantic with grief and filled Your ears with her moaning and complaints because You seemed to treat her tears so lightly, when in fact You were using my own desires to snatch me away for the healing of those desires.** (5/8/15, pp. 84–85)

We can distinguish

(1) Desires and deeds that are sinful,

(2) Desires and deeds that are perfect,

(3) Desires and deeds that are not sinful but yet not perfect in faith, hope, and charity.

Monica's tears came from category (3), not from category (2). But God used them, even so. God even used category (1), Augustine's own sinful desires and deeds, to save him eventually *from* sinful desires and deeds, as he says in his last line; so how much more would He not use Monica's category (3) tears? He uses imperfect things to get perfect things in the end. In His perfect economy, nothing is wasted.

What is really a straight line, the shortest distance between two points, may appear as a curved and twisted line to us, because we are living in curved space-time, not in the timeless abstract concepts of Euclidean geometry. In our world, in which physical relativity reigns, a sufficient amount of matter can curve space, so that what we expect to be the straightest line or the shortest time is really not. It is not unreasonable to expect something analogous in divine Providence.

God was in fact not ignoring Monica's tears or treating them more lightly than Monica was. He was making the same "psychoanalytic" distinction, within those tears, that was explained in the previous passage: the distinction between (1) the essence, or the depth, of them and of the heart's desires from which they flowed and (2) the surface feelings and thoughts of which Monica was aware. Those tears were precious and powerful prayers because they flowed not just from the surface but from deep faith and love in the depth of her heart that God alone knew. But her moanings and complaints flowed partly from a lack of faith, a lack of perfect trust, in her surface consciousness. (Even saints are far from perfect and are the first to admit it.) God rejected the surface but accepted the depth. He rejected the surface precisely *because* He accepted the depths. He did not ignore either of those two dimensions of her tears. He is not a Stoic. He does not ignore hurt feelings just because they are not perfect. He weeps with us (actively, not passively) and waits with us, because He *is* with us, even in our foolish Monican moanings.

Skeptical Doubts

> **The notion began to grow in me that the philosophers whom they call Academics** [skeptics] **were wiser than the rest, because they held that everything should be treated as a matter of doubt and affirmed that no truth can be understood by men.** (5/10/19, p. 87)

Skepticism is a perennial danger at any stage in the search for truth, because it amounts to giving up, despair, hopelessness. After many failures, it is a natural temptation simply to give up the search for truth and declare that *that* is the only truth we can know: that we cannot attain the truth, "true truth", objective truth, with any surety or certainty. Skepticism says, "I've finally found the truth: that truth can't be found. And that's the only truth that can be found." Skepticism thus can look like making a success out of your very failure. It also flatters your pride, because most people are not skeptics, and you can now look down on them as naïve and simplistic.

In his later work, "Against the Skeptics", Augustine uses two very simple arguments against skepticism, one negative, one positive. The negative one is that skepticism refutes itself; it is logically self-contradictory, for it says that it is true that there is no truth, that we know that we cannot know. The positive one is that we simply *cannot* doubt that we exist, that we live, and that we think; for in order to doubt, you must exist and live and think. (Descartes, unlike Augustine, used this point as the fulcrum or foundation or first premise for the whole of his philosophical system.)

> **When I desired to think of my God, I could not think of Him save as a bodily magnitude, for it seemed to me that what was not such was nothing at all. . . . Because of this I thought that the substance of evil was in some sense similar, and had its own hideous and formless bulk, either gross . . . or thin and tenuous like the air: for they imagine it to be some malignant mind creeping over the earth. And because such poor piety as I had constrained me to hold that the good God could not have created any nature evil, I supposed that there were two opposing powers, each infinite, yet the evil one lesser and the good one greater.** (5/10/19–20, pp. 87–88)

Descartes begins his philosophy with universal methodic doubt, then overcomes it with his "I think, therefore I am." But there are three great difference between Descartes' doubt and Augustine's. First, Descartes' doubt is only methodological, the first step in his scientific method. Augustine is a lover, not a scientist. Second, Descartes' doubt is merely intellectual, while Augustine's is lived, and it hurts. Augustine is a lover, not a rationalist. Third, Descartes doubts whether we can know any truth in general, while Augustine doubts whether we can know *God*. His whole philosophy is a search for God, not just for abstract truth. Augustine is a lover, not a professor.

Pascal (one of Augustine's greatest disciples) noted that our imagination usually dominates our reason. That was

Augustine's difficulty in thinking about God. We can only imagine things in space and time, but God is in neither. The same is true of good and evil: they are literally unimaginable.

But although Augustine's mind was on the wrong track here, his heart and conscience were on the right track in insisting that "the good God could not have created any nature evil." Whatever God is, He is good. So if evil is a thing (which was the only thing Augustine could imagine it to be at the time), then the good God did not create it, and so there must also be another Creator of it, an evil God—and that is why Manicheeism, with its theology of the two Gods, seemed the only possible answer to the problem of evil. Like most errors, it was based on a true premise (the good God does not create evil) combined with a false one (evil is a thing).

Saint Ambrose versus Manicheeism

The Manichees claimed that they were the true Christians and that the Catholic Church and her Scriptures had perverted the original true teaching of Christ. (This is the same historical claim that is made both by Muslims and Modernists like the "Jesus Seminar".) So to be a Manichee seemed to have the triple advantage of solving the problem of evil, being a Christian, and being not just an ordinary simple believer but an elite, sophisticated, up-to-date, scientific one. (It was, of course, really pseudo-sophisticated and pseudo-scientific as well as pseudo-Christian.)

However, Augustine soon found a problem in the Manichean claim to be true, original Christianity:

> **I thought it quite impossible to defend certain things which the Manichees had criticized in Your Scriptures: but I did by now quite honestly desire to discuss these things one by one with someone learned in Scripture and find out what he made of them. For the speech of one Elpidius, who had spoken and disputed face to face against the Manichees, had already begun to affect me at Carthage, when he produced arguments from Scripture which were not easy to answer. And the answer they gave seemed to me feeble —indeed they preferred not to give it in public but only among ourselves in private—the answer being that the Scriptures of the New Testament had been**

> **corrupted by some persons unknown who wished to graft the law of the Jews upon the Christian faith; yet the Manicheans made no effort to produce uncorrupted copies.** (5/11/21, pp. 88–89)

Elpidius' argument was very simple, and it remains the essential argument of orthodox Christians against Modernists today. The Modernists, like the Manichees, claim that the Bible we have today gives us, not the real historical Jesus, but a later myth—in other words, they claim that "the historical Jesus" is not identical with "the Christ of (the Catholic) faith". The refutation of this claim is the simple fact that there is not one shred of real evidence for any other, earlier "historical Jesus" than the one in the New Testament. All the heretical versions come later: Gnostic gospels, Manicheeism, Islam, and Modernism. There is also no evidence within the New Testament of any distinction between an earlier, historically accurate layer and a later, mythical layer. That distinction is wholly imposed on the text from without, from the prejudices of those who dislike something in it. In the case of Manicheeism, it is Jesus' Judaism and the doctrine that the good God created matter and declared it good. In the case of Modernism, it is Jesus' divine identity, miracles, and Resurrection—in other words, the whole supernatural dimension. In the case of Islam, it is the idea that Jesus, whom they regard as a great prophet, was allowed by Allah to be publicly disgraced and crucified and also the idea that He claimed divinity. All three of these heretical theologies explain the contradictions between their teachings and those of the New Testament by claiming that the New Testament we have is a later, corrupted version. But "they made no effort to produce uncorrupted copies." How could they? They did not exist.

Now skeptical of Manicheeism, Augustine wants to give Catholic Christianity another try and tries to interview Bishop Ambrose, who already has a reputation for great wisdom and sanctity.

> **I could not ask of him** [Ambrose] **what I wished as I wished, for I was kept from any face to face conversation with him by the throng of men with their own troubles, whose infirmities he served. The very little time he was not with these he was refreshing either his body with necessary food or his mind with reading.** (6/3/3, p. 97)

How shy and sensitive Augustine is! This "throng of men . . . whose infirmities he served" had no qualms about imposing on the bishop's precious time, but Augustine did. The next sentence implies that Augustine watched him from a distance, not daring to talk to him:

> **When he read, his eyes travelled across the page and his heart sought into the sense, but voice and tongue were silent.** (6/3/3, pp. 97–98)

What is remarkable to us is that it was remarkable to Augustine that Ambrose read silently. This was almost unheard of in ancient times. For most premoderns, writing was related to speech as sheet music was related to music. Only a Beethoven could hear in his head every sound of the orchestra when he read a piece of sheet music, and only an Ambrose could hear the words in his mind that he did not hear his tongue pronounce. This difference between the ancients and moderns is not accidental and peripheral but quite deep. We have a very different relationship to language than our ancestors had because we have abstracted meaning from sound. We are far more cerebral and abstract than our ancestors, who were by nature more sacramental. Our minds are more like computers than like the minds of animals.

That fact also explains why Augustine, though a genius, had such great difficulty rising above his concrete imagination when trying to think of the nature of God. As the next excerpt shows:

> **I heard him every Sunday preaching the word of truth to his congregation; and I . . . learned that the phrase, "man created by You in Your own image", was not taken by Your spiritual children . . . to mean that You are bounded within the shape of a human body. And although I had not the vaguest or most shadowy notion how a spiritual substance could be, yet I was filled with shame—but joyful too—that I had been barking all these years not against the Catholic faith but against mere figments of carnal imaginations.** (6/3/4, p. 98)

Fulton Sheen said that he never met an atheist, that is, someone who denied the God of the Catholic Faith, but it was always another god that was denied, confused with the real one. To know the real God is to love Him, to trust Him, and to believe in Him. That's why in Heaven, though all have free will, no one ever doubts, despairs, or sins. And if to know Him is to believe in Him, then not to believe in Him must be not to know Him, to misunderstand Him.

Augustine's specific misunderstanding is instructive. We may think he is very childish and "primitive" in having thought that Christians worshipped a God with literal hands and eyes. But there are two reasons why we should reverse this judgment and question ourselves instead; for perhaps even the preconversion Augustine knew something that we have largely forgotten.

First, God does indeed have real hands and eyes from all eternity. They are just not the physical hands and eyes of Christ's human nature. Our hands are finite symbols of His infinite power, our eyes finite symbols of His infinite knowledge. Our hands and eyes are the image of His, not vice versa.

And second, our "correct" idea of God as immaterial spirit can be even more misleading than the "primitive" idea of God. For in affirming that God is *immaterial*, we may imply that He is, in effect, *impersonal*—which would be the far greater error. Physical human persons are made in His image; abstract, spiritual principles are not. God is indeed spirit, not matter; but God is also person. And that is much more important. "Impersonal spirit" is farther from God than "embodied person".

The fact that Augustine rejoices in the fact that he had been in error is significant. He is not egotistically attached to his own opinions; he is open to truth wherever it is; he has *hope* that the Catholic Faith might be true even before he has *faith* that it is.

This is a very practical point for apologetics. Tolkien calls the Gospel the world's greatest fairy tale, something all good men wish were true. ("On Fairy Stories"). If that wish, that love from the heart, comes first, then the mind's belief will more readily follow. Pascal says that the apologist should first address the heart and explain how Christianity is something we naturally wish were true even if we believe it isn't. That way, the heart can lead and instruct the head; love and beauty can pave the way for truth.

It does this, *not* by inserting a subjective emotion between the mind and objective truth by some "wishful thinking" ("I want it to be true, therefore it is"), but by *removing* the emotional obstacles of hate and fear; not by clouding the mind, but by clearing it, by clearing away misunderstandings. That is what Ambrose did for Augustine.

Wisdom from a Drunken Beggar

I was preparing an oration in praise of the Emperor in which I was to utter any number of lies to win the applause of people who knew they were lies. . . . I was passing along a certain street in Milan when I noticed a beggar. He was jesting and laughing and I imagine more than a little drunk. I fell into gloom and spoke to the friends who were with me about the endless sorrows that our own insanity brings us: for here was I striving away, dragging the load of my unhappiness under the spurring of my desires, and making it worse by dragging it: and with all our striving, our one aim was to arrive at some sort of happiness without care: the beggar had reached the same goal before us, and we might quite well never reach it at all. The very thing that he had attained by means of a few pennies begged from passers-by —namely the pleasure of a temporary happiness—I was plotting for with so many a weary twist and turn. Certainly his joy was no true joy; but the joy I sought in my ambition was emptier still. In any event he was cheerful and I worried, he had no cares and I nothing but cares. (6/6/9, p. 102)

A chance encounter can occasion a sudden life-changing insight. The cheery drunk Augustine met in the street introduced no new fact into Augustine's mental universe—he had always known that such people existed—but it challenged him to compare his own life with the drunk's and that catalyzed a "know thyself" moment. Similarly, Augustine had always known that young people sometimes die suddenly, but his close friend's death had been a life-changing experience for him.

Why did this little encounter cut so deep? Because of Augustine's passion for joy. All seek joy, or deep happiness. And this happiness has both a subjective, felt dimension and an objective, true dimension. Augustine said of the drunk's happiness: "Certainly his joy was no true joy" objectively; but neither was Augustine's vain life of intellectual prostitution, selling his mind rather than his body, flattering corrupt politicians with sophistic rhetoric. Meanwhile, the drunk had at least a felt, temporary happiness, which Augustine and his pagan friends lacked.

His critique of his "life-style" here is similar to his earlier critique of his education as a child. Adults had forced him to give up the joys of play in exchange for hard study—why? So that by study he could grow up to be successful, i.e., get a well-paying job—why? So that he could do what he wanted with his life—which was to play. But he was doing that already as a child! Similarly, the drunken beggar had already reached at least the subjective half of the goal Augustine was presently struggling so unhappily to attain.

It is embarrassing for adults to realize how stupid they are. One of the reasons Augustine is so unusually profound and original is that he cuts through the false modesty of adult superiority.

Augustine's dissatisfaction with his own life was a necessary preliminary to his conversion. Someone who is totally satisfied with his life is not going to convert, or marry, or join the army. (For conversion is very much like marrying or joining the army.)

Folly in the Arena

[Augustine's young, innocent friend Alypius] **had been carried away by an incredible passion for gladiatorial shows. He had turned from such things and utterly detested them. But it happened one day that he met some friends and fellow-students coming from dinner: and though he flatly refused and vigorously resisted, they used friendly violence and forced him along with them to the amphitheatre on a day of these cruel and murderous Games. He protested "Even if you drag my body to the place, can you force me to turn my mind and my eyes on the show? Though there, I shall not be there, and so I shall defeat both you and it." Hearing this his companions led him on all the faster, wishing to discover whether he could do as he had said. When they had reached the arena and had got such seats as they could, the whole place was in a frenzy of hideous delight. He closed up the door of his eyes and forbade his mind to pay attention to things so evil. If only he could have stopped his ears too! For at a certain critical point in the fight, the vast roar of the whole audience beat upon him. His curiosity got the better of him, and thinking that he would be able to treat the sight with scorn—whatever the sight might be—he opened his eyes and was stricken with a deeper wound in the soul than the man whom he had opened his eyes to see got in the body. . . . He drank in all the frenzy . . . and was drunk with**

lust for blood. He was no longer the man who had come there but one of the crowd. (6/8/13, p. 105)

Alypius was Augustine's opposite: sexually innocent but addicted to the pornography of violence. Because the addict is addicted, he is in love with his addiction; but because he knows he is addicted, he is at the same time disgusted with it because he knows it is destroying him and his freedom.

Just as Augustine's friends put "pear pressure" on him to steal pears and put social pressure on him to share their sexual "conquests", Alypius' "friends" pressured him to share their indulgence in the spectacle of torture and murder that was the gladiatorial contests, which were held in every large Roman city.

Alypius, more naïve than Augustine, is confident of his power to resist the temptation and, predictably, falls, since "pride goeth before a fall"—a fall, Augustine notes, that was a more serious and mortal wound in his soul than the dying gladiator got in his body. Mother Teresa shared Augustine's priorities when she said that mothers who abort their unborn children do more harm to their own souls than they do to their babies' bodies.

What is the attractiveness of inhuman "games" like these? We are hard-wired to find joy only in self-transcendence, in self-forgetful love, and even mystical experience. Losing your ego and conscience during mass hysteria like this, like drugs, sex, and frenzied rock concerts, apes the mystical self-forgetfulness and self-transcendence in God for which we are all designed. But Alypius lost himself, not to God, but to "the crowd". How very modern!

Time and Procrastination

I was much exercised in mind as I remembered how long it was since that nineteenth year of my age in which I first felt the passion for true knowledge and resolved that when I found it I would give up all the empty hopes and lying follies of vain desires. And here I was going on thirty, still sticking in the same mire, greedy for the enjoyment of things present though they ever eluded me and wasted my soul, and at every moment saying: "Tomorrow I shall find it. . . . And those mighty Academics—is it true that nothing can be grasped with certainty for the directing of life? No: we must search the more closely and not despair. For now the things in the Scriptures which used to seem absurd are no longer absurd. . . . I shall set my foot upon that step on which my parents placed me as a child, until I clearly find the truth. But where shall I search? When shall I search? Ambrose is busy. I am myself too busy to read. . . . My pupils occupy the morning hours, but what do I do with the rest? Why not do this? But if I do, when shall I have time to visit the powerful friends of whose influence I stand in need, or when prepare the lessons I sell to my pupils, or when refresh myself by relaxing my mind . . . .

"But perish all this. Let me dismiss this vanity and emptiness and give myself wholly to the search for

> **truth. Life is a poor thing, death may come at any time: if it were to come upon me suddenly, in what state should I depart this life? . . .**
>
> **"Yet stay a moment. After all, these worldly things are pleasant, they have their own charm and it is no small charm. . . ."**
>
> **These things went through my mind, and the wind blew one way and then another, and tossed my heart this way and that. Time was passing and I delayed to turn to the Lord. From day to day I postponed life in You, but I did not postpone the death that daily I was dying in myself.** (6/11/18–19, pp. 108–10)

> **I was in love with the idea of happiness, yet I feared it where it was, and fled away from it in my search for it. The plain truth is that I thought I should be impossibly miserable if I had to forego the embraces of a woman: and I did not think of Your mercy as a healing medicine for that weakness, because I had never tried it. I thought that continency was a matter of our own strength, and I knew that I had not the strength: for in my utter foolishness I did not know the word of Your Scripture that none can be continent unless You give it. And truly You would have given it if with groaning of spirit I had assailed Your ears and with settled faith had cast my care upon You.** (6/11/19, p. 110)

Time is the horizon, the dividing line, between God and everything else. Only God is timeless. Our soul is as much in time as our body. Of itself, it is in spiritual time (*kairos*), and by being the form of the body, the life of the body, it is also subject to material time (*kronos*). That is why Augustine finds memory so important (book 10): it transcends *kronos* and makes the dead past mentally come alive in the present. That is also why Augustine spends so much time speculating about how God created angels and the material universe (books 11–13). That is the connection between this most abstract issue (what is time?) and the utterly concrete story of his life that is the plot line of the *Confessions*: because that story is the story of the interaction between eternity and time, between God and Augustine, between grace and nature, between Providence and free will—and *that* is the central plot line of his whole story (and ours).

It is time that allows us to run away from God by procrastination, which is what Augustine is confessing here. In books 11–13, he will investigate its universal philosophical principles; here, he keenly observes the particular details of its practical psychology. His reading of Cicero's *Hortensius* had been the occasion for his "first conversion", if not to God personally, then at least to the absolute authority and desirability of a divine attribute, eternal truth. He now remembers that he has been dithering and procrastinating for eleven years, with his nose to the grindstone of temporal, worldly goods instead of pursuing the eternal truth that Cicero had shown him. (Meeting the drunken beggar probably triggered this self-doubt.)

He could procrastinate, but he could not forget and bury Cicero's challenge entirely in his heart. His conscience accused him and made him give excuses, however silly, for his procrastination. They amounted to one word: the dangerous word "tomorrow". (Remember Macbeth's famous "tomorrow and tomorrow and tomorrow" speech, uttered by a damned soul who has lost all hope.) "Don't stop thinking about tomorrow" is one of the most idiotic pieces of advice that has ever become the title of a popular song (and a political party's deliberately chosen campaign song, no less, back in 1992). For this is exactly that the Devil wants us to do. The future is the least real of the three dimensions of time. For the past is rock-solidly real and unchangeable, and the present is alive; the future is neither. In the wise words of an orange-haired teenage female philosopher named Annie, "Tomorrow is always a day away." So if you want to push God or truth or Heaven away, "tomorrow" is a very convenient category in which to put it. It is a kind of cage or lock box or freezer.

Notice how Augustine's two minds, the wise mind that lives in the present and thinks about the present and the foolish mind that doesn't stop thinking about tomorrow, argue with each other. *Kairos* is always about present action; it is "time for" something. *Kronos* is purely theoretical, speculative, passive, and impersonal; it is not human time but calendar time, clock time. We all have these two minds, parallel to these two kinds of time; but Augustine, more self-aware and demanding than most of us, habitually conducts a dialogue with himself and questions himself. And in entering into a dialogue with his deeper mind, he also engages in a dialogue with God, even though only anonymously.

Notice also how Augustine's wise mind brings up the one fact about ourselves that is not only absolutely certain but also almost forces us to think wisely about ourselves and about eternity: the fact that we are going to die. In fact, we are dying *now*, however slowly.

Augustine's substitution of abstract *kronos* time for concrete *kairos* time feeds, and is fed by, his substitution of an abstract concept of happiness for a concrete one. He loved "the idea of" happiness in the abstract but feared it where it concretely was (in God and in the Church). That is like loving "the idea of Humanity" but hating your next-door neighbor—an unfortunately easy and common practice.

Then, finally, after all this puffing and profundity, Augustine comes down to the real "bottom line". The reason he did not want to become a Christian was that he did not want to reform his sex life. The rest is all excuses and window dressing.

Unlike most Christians today, Augustine the pagan knew quite clearly what the Church demanded of those who would follow Christ: either continence or marriage. And he wanted neither. He did not want to give up his mistress, because he could not even imagine curbing his libido; and he did not want to marry her either, probably for reasons of social class, prestige, and career. (Which of those two reasons, the hot one or the cold one, is the worse one is a question the Devil likes us to ask so that we can feel self-righteous about the other one.)

Nothing makes Augustine more obviously a man of our time than this sexual slavery. Each person, each culture, and each age has its idol, its alternative god, its preferred absolute. Ours, like his, is the demand for sexual autonomy—and therefore slavery.

There is one big difference between his age and ours, though. Augustine and his age were clear about what Christ demanded, about the impossibility of just adding a "faith dimension" to a pagan life-style without any radical change or sacrifice. The majority of Christians in Western civilization today do not even hear what the Church demands in the area of sexual morality, and certainly they do not understand the reasons behind it, the "big picture". That's why most Christians in the West do not even *try* to live the distinctive Christian life in this area any more. Christians fornicate, adulterate, divorce, contracept, sodomize, and abort at nearly the same rate as anyone else.

> **Such honour as there is in marriage from the duty of well-ordered life together and the having of children, had very small influence with . . . us. What held me so fiercely bound was principally the sheer habit of sating a lust that could never be satisfied.** (6/12/22, p. 111)

Augustine does not defend but merely confesses his personal rejection of the married state for himself. He knows it is an honorable state. Why then did he reject it? Because he was judging marriage through the eyes of lust rather than lust through the eyes of marriage.

And lust, like all addictions, demands an ever-increasing exertion for an ever-decreasing "high". This process is hopeless because, unlike both marriage and religion (faith, hope, and charity), it has no end, no peace, no satisfaction. It is a foretaste (and warning) of Hell, where our desires can "never be satisfied" and pour themselves out into nothingness forever.

The Problem of Evil

> **I was so gross of mind—not even seeing myself clearly—that whatever was not extended in space . . . I thought must be nothing whatsoever. My mind was in search of such images as the forms my eye was accustomed to see; and I did not realise that the mental act by which I formed these images was not itself a bodily image.** (7/1/2, pp. 117–18)

Here Augustine for the first time mentions the philosophical breakthrough that definitively refuted the materialism that was at the root of all three of Augustine's major intellectual objections to Christianity: the nature of God, the problem of evil, and the apparent relativity of morals. The objects of the imagination are limited to things that have matter and space; and neither God's omnipresence nor evil's negative reality nor morality's abstract, unchangeable principles can be objects of the imagination.

The refutation of this materialism is simple. The materialist denies spiritual reality and reduces spiritual concepts to sensory images; but even the sensory imagination is an act or power of consciousness and is not itself sensorially imaginable. The objects of the imagination have shape and color, but what shape or color is the act of imagining?

The imagination cannot imagine itself. The understanding, however, can understand itself. We can have a concept of the act of conceiving, and we can also have a concept of the act of imagining. Indeed, even the materialist has such a concept, because the word "imagining" is meaningful to him. But this conceptualizing transcends materialism. The light of the projection machine must transcend the images it projects on the screen. A material image cannot create an image; only an immaterial soul can. (Even animals have somewhat immaterial souls. They are not machines. They have imaginations.)

It is exceedingly strange that many otherwise intelligent philosophers today simply cannot see this point when they embrace a materialist "solution" to the "mind-body problem".

> **I sought for the origin of evil, but I sought in an evil manner.** (7/5/7, p. 121)

Augustine is truly a Socratic thinker: he never forgets "know thyself." He does this both theoretically, when he refutes materialism by remembering that his mind that projects material images is not itself material or imaginable (the excerpt above), and also practically, here, when he remembers that the person who is trying to solve the "problem of evil" is an evil person. In other words, evil is what Gabriel Marcel famously called a "mystery" rather than a "problem", a question from which we cannot detach ourselves but in which we are so involved that we create the "problem" in the very act of confronting it. To see the "problem of evil", use not a telescope but a mirror. It's closer than you think. The same is true of the "mind-body problem". We cannot transcend it and solve it because we *are* it.

> **Where then is evil, and what is its source, and how has it crept into the creation? What is its root, what**

> **is its seed? Can it be that it is wholly without being? But why should we fear and be on guard against what is not? Or if our fear of it is groundless, then our very fear is itself an evil thing. For by it the heart is driven and tormented for no cause; and that evil is all the worse, if there is nothing to fear yet we do fear. Thus either there is evil which we fear, or the fact that we fear is evil.** (7/5/7, p. 121)

Atheists routinely use evil to disprove God; for if there is an all-good God, what room can there be in Him or in His creation for evil? Augustine here considers and rejects an inadequate answer: that evil is an illusion, not a reality. That is, in different ways, the solution of philosophical idealism, some forms of Hinduism and Buddhism, and Mary Baker Eddy's "Christian Science". Its refutation is swift, clean, and merciless, like a sharp sword stroke. If evil does not exist, and "we have nothing to fear but fear itself", things are worse, not better; for we are letting an illusion dominate our lives. FDR's famous saying is self-contradictory.

(When we read an argument like this, we naturally think: How can our minds be so dull as not to see this? Why don't our mental swords cut that cleanly and clearly?)

A similar popular error is the idea that there is no sin and therefore no reason to feel guilty. That just gives us an additional reason to feel guilty! A sinner who feels guilt is at least sane and living in reality; an innocent who feels guilt is out of touch with reality and so is a sinner who feels none.

What Plato Had and What Plato Lacked

The next quotation summarizes the whole relationship between Christianity and the best of pagan Greek philosophy (which, for Augustine, was Plato): both its greatest truth and its greatest lack.

> **You brought in my way . . . some books of the Platonists translated from Greek into Latin. In them I found, though not in the very words, yet the thing itself and proved by all sorts of reasons: that *in the beginning was the Word and the Word was with God and the Word was God; the same was in the beginning with God; all things were made by Him and without Him was made nothing that was made; in Him was life and the life was the light of men, and the light shines in darkness and the darkness did not comprehend it.* . . . But I did not read in those books that *He came unto His own, and His own received Him not, but to as many as received Him He gave power to be made the sons of God, to them that believed in His name.* Again I found in them that the Word, God, was *born not of flesh nor of blood, nor of the will of man nor of the will of the flesh, but of God;* but I did not find that *the Word became flesh.* . . . [T]hese books did not tell me that *He emptied Himself, taking the form of a servant, being made in the likeness of men, and in habit found as a man;* or that *He humbled***

> ***Himself becoming obedient unto death, even to the death of the cross.*** (7/9/13–14; pp. 126–27)

On the basis of his reading of "the Platonists" (probably the later "Neoplatonists"; it is not certain which works of Plato's, if any, Augustine actually read), Augustine imagines Plato reading the first chapter of John's Gospel and saying "That's what I thought, too!" to the first half of it and "That's nowhere near what I thought" to the other half.

Augustine's first point is essentially this: that pagan philosophy at its best, natural human reason at its best, unaided by faith and divine revelation, did in fact come to know, in however vague and confused a way, the nature of God as eternal truth. That was Saint John's point when he wrote that the *Logos*, or eternal Word, the Mind or Reason of God "that enlightens every man was coming into the world" (Jn 1:9). Christ said, "I am . . . the truth" (Jn 14:6), and therefore whenever anyone knows truth, they know Christ.

But they do not know that they know Christ. They know His *what* but not His *who*. They know *of* Him (*wissen*, *savoir*) but they do not know Him (*kennen*, *connaître*).

No human reason, by itself, could have known the Incarnation and the Gospel. Not even God's own chosen people expected that. Probably no angel or Devil did, either. It was, quite literally, the most amazing and startling thing that has ever happened. Kierkegaard calls it "the Absolute Paradox".

There was indeed in paganism at its best a "way up", from the knowledge of Man and Nature to the knowledge of God. Everyone, Gentile as well as Jew, could walk on that road by natural reason (Rom 1:19–20) and conscience (Rom 2:14–15). But no man's mind could know the "way down" from God to Man in Christ. Only the One who said "I AM the way" knew that way. It was a "Him", not an "it". Man could enter it only by faith, by personal trust, not by reason alone.

Those two facts (what Plato knew and what he didn't) are human reason's greatest glory and its greatest failure. Few thinkers, if any, ever saw those two points more clearly and strongly than Augustine.

The Problem of Evil Solved

> **And it became clear to me that corruptible things are good: if they were supremely good they could not be corrupted, but also if they were not good at all they could not be corrupted: if they were supremely good they would be incorruptible, if they were in no way good there would be nothing in them that might corrupt. For corruption damages; and unless it diminished goodness, it would not damage. Thus . . . all things that are corrupted are deprived of some goodness. But if they were deprived of all goodness, they would be totally without being. . . . [T]herefore as long as they are, they are good. Thus whatsoever things are, are good; and that evil whose origin I sought is not a substance, because if it were a substance it would be good.** (7/12/18, p. 130)

"All that is, is good"—this was another breakthrough realization, and Augustine's exit pass out of Manicheeism. Aquinas, eight centuries later, proved its truth by a simple disjunctive syllogism: All that exists is either God the Creator, Who is good, or one of His creatures, all of which He declared good; therefore all that exists, is good.

This cosmic, objective, ontological optimism is quite compatible with a robustly realistic pessimism about man's subjective moral evil and sinfulness. In fact, the former is the ground for judgment on the latter: since both the

Creator and His creatures are good, man's and the angels' sin is the only blemish on God's creation. The greatness of the good defines the greatness of the evil. A patch of mud does little evil to a junkyard but great evil to a beautiful woman's face. Augustine, like Dostoyevsky, stretches us almost unendurably in both directions, the optimistic and the pessimistic.

But there is not only sin, in humans, but also corruption —pain, disease, deformity, and death—in subhuman creatures as well as in us. Is this not also real evil? How then can it be that "all that is, is good"?

Augustine's answer is that "if they were not good at all, they could not be corrupted . . . and unless it damaged goodness, it would not damage." Evil is the lack of good, the privation of good, and this can exist only in something that is good. Evil is real, but it is not a thing, a creature, a being, a "substance", an entity. It is like darkness, which is not a thing like light but is the lack of light. Light is a real thing, but darkness, though real, is not a thing. Cold is not a thing, like heat; it is the absence of heat. There is such a thing as heat (thermal energy), but there is not also another thing called cold energy.

There is an important distinction to be made here: evil is not just an absence but a lack. For instance, blindness is the lack of sight where it ought to be. It is not evil for a rock not to have sight (so we don't call a rock "blind"); but it is evil for a man or an animal to lack sight. And it is not evil for a rock to lack virtue, but it is evil for a man to lack virtue.

Another important distinction is that the lack of physical goods is physical evil; the lack of moral or spiritual goods is moral or spiritual evil.

Augustine does not tell us whether this insight just came to him, suddenly or gradually, or whether Ambrose explained it to him. But once the idea is understood, it seems almost self-evident. What was lacking in Manicheeism's arguments was not logic but understanding.

> **There is no sanity in those whom anything in creation displeases.** (7/14/120, p. 131)

If all things are good, then we are not conforming to reality when we hate any thing, even a hemorrhoid or a Jersey mosquito. One of the implications of the human condition that Christian theology labels "Original Sin" is that we are all quite insane. We alone: Did you ever see baby robins who said "No" to the worms their Mommy gave them to eat?

> **So that when I now asked what is iniquity, I realised that it was not a substance but a swerving of the will which is turned towards lower things and away from You, O God.** (7/16/22, p. 132)

No thing is evil, but some human desires, motives, choices, and actions are. "Iniquity" (sin, moral evil) is real, but it is not a "substance". It is not a thing given to us from the universe, but an act we give into the universe. It is a "swerving of the will" that prefers some lower good, some creature, to God. But the man, the willpower, the mind, the physical act, and the lower good are all ontologically good. You have to be a "good shot" to be an assassin. Even the Devil has to have a powerful intellect and will (which in themselves are good things and created by God) in order to pervert them.

A Mystical Experience

> **And I marvelled to find that at last I loved You and not some phantom instead of You; yet I did not stably enjoy my God, but was ravished to You by Your beauty yet soon was torn away from You again by my own weight, and fell again with torment to lower things. Carnal habit was that weight. Yet the memory of You remained with me and I knew without doubt that it was You to whom I should cleave.** (7/17/23, p. 132)

The ontological "weight" (*pondus*) Augustine speaks of here is a kind of destiny. He writes, *Amor meus, pondus meum*. "My love is my weight", my gravity. I go where my love goes. It pulls me.

But Augustine's heart is divided. It truly loves God, but also "lesser things" in preference to God, i.e., as idols. That is what "carnal habit" means. It doesn't just mean sex, as "flesh" doesn't just mean body. Once he left the Manichees, Augustine never blamed his body for his sins. Sin is "a swerving of the will" and the deeds commanded by the will, a swerving by the musicians from the Conductor's baton and the assigned sheet music.

What would it be like to have an undivided heart, to be one with God and His will? Augustine here confesses an all-too-brief experience of loving and touching (or rather, being touched by) the true God and being "ravished" by

His beauty. (Notice the sexual image!) It left a memory in Augustine's soul, which is so painful that he calls it a "torment". Yet that pain was also incomparable bliss. Perhaps this is a foretaste of Purgatory.

Whether we call this a "mystical" experience is mainly a question about words and labels. Look at the things, not at the words.

This experience also finally gave Augustine certainty ("without doubt"). Why? Such sudden certainty is surprising in a man like Augustine, who is such a passionately questioning and demanding thinker that he habitually doubts every idea that enters his mind. The answer is that this was not just an idea, this was Reality that he touched.

In touching God's goodness in the form of His beauty, Augustine also experienced a foretaste of his own supreme good and Heavenly joy and also his own fundamental earthly purpose, task, and duty: "that it was You to whom I should cleave". To know God without knowing this as our fundamental moral "should" is not to know God. An amoral mysticism is false mysticism. Kierkegaard would classify it as merely "aesthetic" rather than "religious", for the "religious" always includes and fulfills the "ethical" even while transcending it.

I was now studying the ground of my admiration for the beauty of bodies, whether celestial or of earth, and on what authority I might rightly judge of things mutable and say: "This ought to be so, that not so." Enquiring then what was the source of my judgment when I did so judge, I had discovered the immutable and true eternity of truth above my changing mind. (7/17/23, p. 132)

What an unusual question! We all by nature make value judgments about material things, but only a philosophical mind reflects on the *ground* or basis or justification of such judgments. To most of us, it never once in our lives even occurs to us that our value judgments need to have any "ground" at all; they just float like clouds. We just assume, commonsensically, that to save a life is good and to take a life is bad; that a long life is better than a life cut short at an early age; or that the night sky is more beautiful than roadside litter.

Augustine, however, pursues this question and discovers the paradox that the ground is in the sky; that nothing less than eternal, objective truth, outside of and independent of his mind, is necessary to justify any value judgment whatever as objectively true and anything more than a purely personal, subjective preference (justice for you, cannibalism for me, just as it's vanilla for you, chocolate for me). The very idea of progress among the changing things of this world logically presupposes a goal that cannot progress; a truth, a good, an end that is eternal, rigid, unchangeable, and absolute. For if the finish line "progresses" as the runners do, they cannot make progress toward it. If the second baseman picks up second base and runs to third as fast as the runner on first base runs toward second, the runner can never progress to second.

If "progressive" thinkers today do not see this point, that can be only due to fuzzy thinking or to stubborn ideological prejudice. Augustine is both clear and honest enough, and also humble and childlike enough, to see it. It is an implicit recognition of God. For eternal truth is only God without a face.

Augustine now climbs the Jacob's ladder of the mind, rung by rung, and ascends to this God:

> **Thus by stages I passed from [1] bodies to [2] the soul which uses the body for its perceiving, and from this to [3] the soul's inner power, to which the body's senses present external things, as indeed the beasts are able; and from there I passed on to [4] the reasoning power, to which is referred for judgment what is received from the body's senses. This too realised that it was mutable in me, and rose to its own understanding . . . that it might find [5] what light suffused it, when with utter certainty it cried aloud that the immutable was to be preferred to the mutable, and how it had come to know the immutable itself: for if it had not come to some knowledge of the immutable, it could not have known it as certainly preferable to the mutable. Thus in the thrust of a trembling glance my mind arrived at That Which Is.** (7/17/23, pp. 132–33)

Typically modern thinkers seem allergic to the very idea of hierarchy, probably because they confuse the artificial hierarchies that rank people into economic or political classes with the natural hierarchies of the universe. But the obvious reality of a real ontological hierarchy emerges once you see and admit the obvious truths that matter is not really equal to spirit, the unconscious to the conscious, the object judged to the subject judging, or time to eternity.

From step 1 to step 2: Souls are superior to bodies because they give life to bodies, not vice versa. In the broadest sense of the word, "soul" means simply "life", or "that which gives life to a living body". So whatever is alive (plant, animal, or human) has a "soul" in this most rudimentary sense.

From step 2 to step 3: All souls give life to bodies (even plant souls do that), but animal souls also perceive the external world through their physical senses. Augustine does not make this distinction here (between plant and animal souls), but he makes the distinction, within animal souls, between the power of external sensory perception and the internal coordination of these different senses. It is like the difference between the king on the throne and the servants he sends out to report to him what is going on outside the castle.

From step 3 to step 4: Animals cannot reason consciously and logically, only instinctively. Man alone is "the rational animal".

From step 4 to step 5: But even the reasoning power, though it is more immaterial and spiritual than sense perception and transcends space, does not transcend time. Reasoning takes time. It is mutable. But truth is not mutable, and truth alone justifies reasoning. The final step, from level 4 to level 5, is really what Augustine had discovered in the previous quotation, which he called "the true eternity of truth above my changing mind". If this objective truth does not exist to judge subjective thoughts, then we cannot speak of a difference between true thoughts and false thoughts and, therefore, between the thought that there is and the thought that there is not such a difference.

Augustine calls this truth "That Which Is" to distinguish it from that which *becomes*. It is the distinction between God the Creator and all His creatures. His mind here discovers God, not just as a *belief* (he had that before; he had never been an atheist), but as a *reality*. He touches God with his mind.

What more does he need? Three things: (1) for this to last; (2) to touch God with his heart and will, to give himself wholly to God; and (3) for God to touch him. Actually, in order for (1) and (2) to happen, (3) has to happen first. That is the essence of Augustine's theology of grace.

> **But I lacked the strength to hold my gaze fixed, and my weakness was beaten back again so that I returned to my old habits, bearing nothing with me but a memory of delight and a desire as for something of which I had caught the fragrance but which I had not yet the strength to eat.** (7/17/23, p. 133)

Clearly Augustine was speaking of something more than the correct *idea* of God in the previous quotation. For no one lacks the power to think of an idea again once he has thought of it the first time, but Augustine says about this (the level (5) that he reached in the previous quotation) that he "lacked the strength to hold my gaze fixed".

Augustine calls it a "gaze". It is an analogy, for he speaks here of the inner eye, not the outer. The old word for this was "contemplation". We all too often think of the mind as something like a computer rather than something like an eye; as a power that receives and stores information and calculates rather than as a power that *sees*, that sees realities, not just ideas. This "contemplation" is not something only monks and mystics do. It is something we all do. We all *see* with the mind as well as the eye. But we don't all see that we see, as Augustine does.

All who have practiced "contemplation" have testified that it is "delightful" and self-justifying, worth doing simply for its own sake. We moderns do not know this joy because we rush past this stage in our thinking without lingering there.

This contemplation that transcends time as it stands *between* the two temporal processes of discovering a first truth and moving on to discover a second. But we must pass through it, even if we do not notice it, as we must pass through the trans-linguistic understanding of a speech in one language in order to translate it into another language, or as we must pass through the notion of infinity in order to compare two finite numbers as closer or farther from this touchstone (e.g., three is one closer to infinity than two). We do not linger lovingly to contemplate and appreciate what we already have.

On the practical level, too, we limit ourselves to the temporal and changing, for we act as if we believed the insane philosophy that the whole meaning of life was not to enjoy any present good that we already have acquired but only to get new ones. Our god is the clock. It is a tyrannical and joyless god.

But if we taste one second of contemplative joy, one "timeless moment", we cannot forget it. We know that it is what we are meant for and what alone can give peace to our "restless heart". Once you have had the tiniest taste of eternity, you cannot be wholly satisfied by any other food. It is a divine gift, an appetizer of Heaven.

Is this "mystical"? Most people would use that label. You may use the word as you please, but if this is mystical, every one of us is meant to be a mystic.

Christianity versus Platonism

> **So I set about finding a way to gain the strength that was necessary for enjoying You. And I could not find it until I embraced the *Mediator between God and man, the man Christ Jesus.*** (7/18/24, p. 133)

Augustine now understands two things: the reality of God and the demands of his own heart, which cannot be satisfied with anything less than God. Wise men of all religions know these two truths in some form, however confused their notion of God may be. But there is a third truth that only Christians know: the Mediator, the connector, the way, the road. Once you see how Godlike God is, you then confront the essential human *koan* puzzle: you *have* to have God, get to God, know God, taste God, or touch God; but you *can't* have God, get to God, know God, taste God, or touch God. The most important goal of all is also the most impossible. "You can't get there from here." The gap is infinite. The road is infinitely long.

In Hinduism, thousands of years of inner psychological explorations of the human heart have crystallized the following conclusion, called "the four wants of man". Every heart has four wants, each deeper than the one before it: for (1) pleasure, (2) power, (3) philanthropy, and (4) Godlikeness, i.e., infinite life, infinite understanding, and infinite bliss (*sat*, *chit*, and *ananda*). We can attain the first three of "the four wants of man" by our own power, but not the fourth. The Hindu answer to this *koan* is the pantheistic doctrine that we are all already there, that we *are* God (*tat tvam asi*, "*Thou art That*"). The Christian answer is radically different: that we are separated from God (by sin) and that only Christ can reunite us. (Sin is not only moral, it is also ontological. It is not only disobedience but divorce.)

Plato helped to show Augustine his goal, eternal truth. But only Christ could show him the way to that goal. Plato gave him a map but not a vehicle for the journey.

Just as a bridge, in order to join the two banks of a river, has to touch both banks, so in order to join God and man, Christ must be both God and man.

Who else even claimed to be that? Krishna and the other Hindu "avatars" are all divine, but not human; in fact for Hinduism what seems to be man is only God in disguise, like the consecrated Host. On the other hand Buddha, Confucius, Lao Tzu, Moses, Zoroaster, and Socrates all claimed to be only men, not God. Christ is utterly unique in claiming to be both: "Son of God" and "son of man". However far "the anonymous Christ" or "the universal Christ" does or does not extend into other religions (and we don't really know the answer to that question with certainty, do we?), there is no second Christ. And we do know *that* with certainty, don't we? His claim is unique, and uniquely polarizing. For if He is not "*the* way" as He claims to be, then he is not any way to God at all, but only an incredibly arrogant egotist. If He is not "the truth" itself, then he is not true at all, but the world's biggest liar. And if He is not "the life" itself of God, then it is not life, holiness, and Heaven that he deals to us, but death, blasphemy, and Hell.

> **I was not yet lowly enough to hold the lowly Jesus as my God, nor did I know what lesson His embracing of our weakness was to teach. For Your Word . . . built for Himself here below a lowly house of our clay, that by it He might bring down from themselves and bring up to Himself those who were to be made subject, healing the swollenness of their pride and fostering their love: so that their self-confidence might grow no further but rather diminish, seeing the deity at their feet, humbled by the assumption of our coat of human nature: to the end that weary at last they might cast themselves down upon His humanity and rise again in its rising.** (7/18/24, pp. 133–34)

What kept Augustine from Christ at this point was a sin infinitely more dangerous than lust. It was pride, a pride that *must* be broken in all of us before salvation or Heaven or union with God is even possible. Humility and honesty are the two virtues that are an absolutely necessary preliminary to all the others.

What can I add to this shattering quotation of Augustine's? I despair of adding anything but dull words of my own that only muffle his music, like layers of snowflakes on a bell. Please just read it again, slowly and aloud, and let God use it to speak to your heart and your honesty.

> **I think it was Your will that I should come upon these books before I had made study of the Scriptures, that . . . I might be able to discern the difference that there is between presumption and confession, between those who see what the goal is but do not see the way, and** [those who see] **the Way which**

> **leads to that country of blessedness, which we are meant not only to know but to dwell in.** (7/20/26, pp. 135–36)

Augustine states in several ways the same essential difference between the philosophical writings of the Platonists, which represented for him the best that paganism could do, and the Christian religion of the Bible.

(1) It is the difference between "presumption" and "confession", i.e., between the presumption of having successfully attained philosophical truth and the confession of our sin and our inability to cure it and to attain Heaven by ourselves;

(2) It is the difference between knowing the goal (eternal truth, the nature of God, and ultimate Heavenly beatitude) but not the way (Christ, divine revelation), and knowing both the goal and the way;

(3) Implicitly contained in (2) is also the difference between "knowing" an impersonal truth (with the mind) and knowing a Person (with the whole self, with the heart).

(4) It is the difference between seeing that goal from afar but not being able to "dwell" (live) in it, and being able to live in it because of this personal knowledge of Him who is the way to it.

All four differences are aspects or dimensions of one difference.

This is the difference between the two most influential human beings who have ever lived, Socrates and Jesus. (Plato was to Socrates what Augustine was to Jesus.)

It is also the difference between philosophy and religion.

To some (hyper-conservatives), the controversial point in what Augustine says here will be his compliment to Plato for knowing so much and coming so close to Christianity. To others (hyper-liberals), it will be Augustine's insult to Plato for knowing so little and for remaining so very far from Christianity.

> **So now I seized greedily upon the adorable writings of Your Spirit, and especially upon the Apostle Paul. . . . In that pure eloquence I saw One Face.** (7/21/27, p. 136)

Here is the fundamental thing Augustine lacked when he read and rejected the Bible earlier. It was his not knowing (*kennen, connaître*) the "One Face" that that whole book reveals, Jesus Christ, the human face of God. Every syllable in that book is a molecule in His face. Reading the Bible without knowing Him is like looking at all the details of a painting of a human face but not recognizing it as a face.

This is why simple saints like Mother Teresa, who seldom spoke words of more than one syllable, understand Scripture far more profoundly than thousands of the world's greatest theological scholars.

> **The writings of the Platonists contain nothing of all this. Their pages show nothing of the face of that love, the tears of confession, Your sacrifice, an afflicted spirit, a contrite and humbled heart, the salvation of Your people, the espoused city, the promise of the Holy Spirit, the chalice of our redemption. In them no one sings: *Shall not my soul be submitted unto God? From Him is my salvation*. . . . And we hear**

> **no voice calling: *Come unto me, all you that labour. . . . For thou hast hidden these things from the wise and prudent and hast revealed them to the little ones.*** (7/21/27, p. 137)

Here Augustine gives us six more ways of expressing the difference between philosophy and religion mentioned two quotations ago:

(1) Philosophers give us impersonal truth. Christ gives us Himself, His very divine Person, both spiritually (in the New Birth) and materially (on the Cross and in the Eucharist: his body and blood as well as His soul and divinity). Every one of the nine items of content Augustine lists in his second sentence is personal. (Count them!)

(2) Philosophers do not *sing*.

(3) Philosophers, if they do sing, do not sing the song of submission and surrender.

(4) Philosophers do not promise salvation (from sin and death and Hell).

(5) Humble and honest philosophers, like Socrates and Buddha, say "Look not to me, look to my teaching." Christ says: "Come unto me." Socrates says, "Think for yourself", and Buddha says: "Be lamps unto yourselves." Christ says: "I am the light of the world."

(6) Philosophers (rightly) try to be wise and prudent, because they are in the presence of, and speaking to, the unwise and imprudent world. Christians try to be humble "little ones", because they are in the presence of their all-wise Heavenly Father.

> **It is one thing to see the land of peace from a wooded mountaintop, yet not find the way to it and struggle hopelessly far from the way, with hosts of those fugitive deserters from God, under their leader the Lion and the Dragon, besetting us about and ever lying in wait; and quite another to hold to the way that leads there.** (7/21/27, p. 137)

And here is a final difference: only Christ works. Only He gets us to God. Only He conquers our enemy the Devil ("the Dragon").

If that's not really true, then the whole thing is a supercolossal fraud. It's either Everything or Nothing. It's not "nice". It's not "values". It's eternal salvation.

The Romans 7 Experience

I was bound not with the iron of another's chains, but by my own iron will. (8/5/10, p. 148)

The enemy within is more dangerous than the enemy without. It seems impossible to escape him. For while it is logically possible for you to escape any *other*, it is not logically possible for you to escape yourself, unless the Law of Identity is revoked.

But perhaps the enemy within is not your very self. That was Saint Paul's solution to the paradox, and Augustine's, too. No pagan thinkers ever reached the depths where they could discover that paradox. The paradox is that "I do not understand my own actions. For I do not do what I want, but I do the very thing I hate. . . . I do not do the good I want, but the evil I do not want is what I do. Now if I do what I do not want, it is no longer I that do it, but sin which dwells within me" (Rom 7:15, 19–20).

Notice that neither Saint Paul nor Saint Augustine blames anything other than his own will. They do not blame God or the Devil or institutions or heredity or environment or fate. They blame themselves. And they do not blame their body, and they do not even blame their passions, for it is the will that is responsible for consenting to or refusing the suggestions of the passions. As Augustine will discover in a little while, just before the famous conversion scene in the garden, the will is not only weak but divided.

Is the will free, then, or bound? Both! No pagan philosopher clearly articulated the doctrine of free will (though Aristotle came close with his distinction between the voluntary and the involuntary), and no pagan philosopher ever discovered the servitude of the will without divine grace.

> **Thus, with myself as object of the experiment, I came to understand what I had read, how the *flesh lusts against the spirit and the spirit against the flesh*.** (8/5/11, p. 148)

In Pauline terminology, "spirit" does not mean "soul", and "flesh" does not mean "body". The distinction Saint Paul makes is not the Manichean one between spirit (= good) and body (= evil). In fact, the worst sins are spiritual sins, and the most evil being in all reality is a pure spirit, the Devil. All matter, on the other hand, is innocent, created by God, and declared good. "Spirit" (*pneuma*), means the whole self under the grace of the Holy Spirit. "Flesh" (*sarx*) means the whole self without grace: fallen, foolish, selfish, and sinful. The word for "soul" is not *pneuma* but *psyche*, and the word for "body" is not *sarx*, but *soma*. When Saint Paul lists "the works of the flesh", he includes spiritual sins like "idolatry, sorcery, enmity, strife, jealousy, anger, selfishness, dissension, party spirit, envy" (Gal 5:20–21). On the other hand, he speaks of a "spiritual *body*" (1 Cor 15:44). And the corporal (bodily) works of mercy are works of the Spirit.

This is life's great battle: not between soul and body, but, within the soul, between Spirit and flesh. Solzhenitsyn famously said that the dividing line between good and evil does not divide races, nations, regimes, or ideologies, but it divides every human heart. It does not run between the external body and the internal soul, or between matter and spirit, as the Manichees said. It is a battle in the human soul and for the human soul between two masters, God and Satan, Heaven and Hell, angels and demons.

Augustine is very clear on this point, both in the *Confessions* and in *The City of God*. The popular image of Augustine is radically wrong. It is that of a Manichean, hating the material world and his own body as the cause of his sins—and, within his sins, concentrating only on his sexual sins. In fact, like his Master, Augustine concentrates his wrath much more on spiritual sins like pride, dishonesty, cowardice, sloth, and procrastination. Perhaps it is his modern critics who are the Manicheans. For they often say they are "spiritual but not religious"; their bookshelves are full of books of "spirituality"; and "sin" is the very last word that would ever spring to their lips.

> **I no longer had the excuse which I used to think I had for not yet forsaking the world and serving You, the excuse namely that I had no certain knowledge of the truth. By now I was quite certain; but I was still bound to earth and refused to take service in Your army.** (8/5/11, p. 148)

The reasons that lead someone to skepticism may be honest (or they may be dishonest), but the *use* that skeptics make of their skepticism is almost always dishonest because it is used as an *excuse*. For knowledge always entails some responsibility to act or live according to that knowledge. Babies are ignorant and, therefore, not responsible. Geniuses and rulers know and, therefore, are responsible for more than ordinary people are. That is the truth behind Augustine's first sentence.

But overcoming skepticism and finding the truth (the first step, which is performed by the mind) is no guarantee that one will accept the truth and live according to it (the second step, which is performed by the will). That is the point of Augustine's second sentence. Especially when the truth is that we must abandon our false gods of this world and risk everything in faith, which is "to take service in Your army". All three kinds of marriage—to a spouse, to an army, and to God—are total risks, in which your entire life is at stake. In the first, you offer at risk your whole heart; in the second, your whole future bodily life; in the third, your eternal soul. It is understandable why skepticism is much more comfortable. We fear to "commit".

> **I was held down as agreeably by this world's baggage as one often is by sleep; and indeed the thoughts with which I meditated upon You were like the efforts of a man who wants to get up but is so heavy with sleep that he simply sinks back into it again. There is no one who wants to be asleep always—for every sound judgment holds that it is best to be awake—yet a man often postpones the effort of shaking himself awake when he feels a sluggish heaviness in the limbs, and settles pleasantly into another doze though he knows he should not, because it is time to get up. . . . For there was nothing I could reply when You called me: *Rise, thou that sleepest and arise from the dead: and Christ shall enlighten thee*; and whereas You showed me by every evidence that Your words were true, there was simply nothing I could answer save only laggard lazy words: "Soon," "Quite soon," "Give me just a little while." But "soon" and "quite soon" did not mean any particular time; and "just**

> **a little while" went on for a long while.** (8/5/12, pp. 148–49)

Fear is a kind of immaterial weight that holds us back from acting. When we are uncertain about the truth, fear of error holds back our mind. When we are certain of the truth but still refuse it, fear of having to give up cherished pleasures holds back our will. When we contemplate marriage, army service, or religious conversion, we fear to give up our creature comforts (pleasures) and the autonomy that lets us control them (power).

When two loves draw us in contrary directions, two corresponding fears hold us back. We act only when one love or one fear outweighs the other. Love is spiritual gravity and fear is spiritual antigravity. Augustine is deeply in love with "this world's baggage", and he knows that on the journey to God you cannot take any baggage with you, not even your right hand or your eye, if that is what holds you back (Mt 5:29–30).

Time, again, is crucial to Augustine. The mind, which deals in eternal truths, has spoken: the Catholic Faith is true. The will, however, deals in temporal actions, and it has not yet followed the mind. Its excuse is not falsehood or uncertainty in the mind but "tomorrowness" in the will and the actions it commands. Truth is timeless, but action is timely and present. "Perhaps" has been overcome by "eternally true" in Augustine's mind; now "tomorrow" and "soon" must be overcome by "now" in his will.

We delight in sleep and in pleasant dreams, such as the dream that the pleasures of this life can go on forever. And we want to postpone the ringing of the alarm clock that tells us that we are asleep and not living in the real world.

We do not like to hear of the obligation of the present moment to get up and deal with our *kairos* time rather than our *kronos*, that is, with concrete real world time rather than abstract imagined time. For *kronos*, tomorrow is just as good a time as today; but this is a lie. *Kairos* tells us the truth: that "there's no time like the present." "Now" is always "the time of salvation" (2 Cor 6:2; Rom 13:11).

Sleep is an image of death. Living in impersonal *kronos* time is like sleeping; that is why God calls us to "Awake, O sleeper, and arise from the dead" (Eph 5:14).

"Now" is always a definite, concrete, specific, real time. "Soon" is an indefinite, abstract, generic, unreal time. It can go on forever, That's what happens in Hell. Hell is like the movie *Groundhog Day*.

> **But You, Lord, . . . turned me back towards myself, taking me from behind my own back where I had put myself all the time that I preferred not to see myself.** (8/7/16, p. 152)

God is like Socrates. (More correctly, Socrates is like God, for God is like nothing, while everything is in different ways a little like Him.) He presses on us with questions. He will not let us escape ourselves, even though we are very clever in finding ways of doing that, in putting ourselves behind our own backs so that we do not see ourselves.

We like to look at ourselves when we are doing something good and honest, but not when we are doing something bad or dishonest. But that is exactly what the Devil wants us to do. Turning from the good thing on which we had focused our attention and back to ourselves makes us self-righteous instead of righteous. To be righteous is to be self-forgetful. And turning from our own dishonesties and sins to focus our attention on the idol we are worshipping makes us self-forgetful instead of humble and repentant. To be humble is to be self-remembering. So God has to undo the Devil's work. He invites us to forget ourselves when we do good, so as not to spoil the good and the joy; and to remember ourselves when we do evil, so that we can "spoil" the evil by acknowledging it and turning from it.

This is the psychology of Augustine and of Christ. Typically modern pop psychology fits in very nicely with the Devil's strategy: the flight from guilt and "judgmentalism" and into self-affirmation, i.e., self-worship. An index of the success of the demonic strategy can be seen in the popular image of Augustine as a miserable man with a terrible "guilt complex".

But if he is so miserable, how was he capable of such joy? The "negative" passages in the *Confessions* can be explained in light of the positive ones, as a negative, "judgmental" x-ray and a sharp and painful scalpel can be explained in light of the healing operation whose result is joy. But the joy cannot be explained in light of the x-ray or the scalpel.

> **And You set me there before my own face that I might see how vile I was, how twisted and unclean and spotted and ulcerous. I saw myself and was horrified; but there was no way to flee from myself. . . . You were setting me face to face with myself, forcing me upon my own sight, that I might see my iniquity and loathe it. I had known it, but I had pretended not to see it, had deliberately looked the other way and let it go from my mind.** (8/7/16, p. 152)

The three things Christ came to save us from are sin, death, and Hell. All three are very painful to behold. We cannot save ourselves from any one of them, but we can save ourselves from the painful sight of them simply by not thinking about them! We cannot cure our diseases, but we can mask their symptoms by simply not admitting them. We can be ostriches.

So we have three and only three options: (1) simply to deny the bad news of sin, (2) to admit the bad news but disbelieve the good news of salvation, or (3) to believe both. The first is dishonest optimism. The second is hopeless pessimism. The third is the only option that is neither dishonest nor hopeless, that admits both sides of the story. And, therefore, it is the only option that is *dramatic*, that produces stories like Augustine's.

When Christianity first came into the world, pessimism was its main rival; today it is optimism. Today we have to preach the bad news before the good news makes any sense. "Free heart transplant!" is not good news to those who think their heart is healthy.

Fortunately, we do not have to hector and moralize. Modern man, by his own admission, is miserable. He already knows his symptoms and can't deny them; all he can deny is the disease that is causing them, namely, sin, i.e., alienation from God, the source of all joy.

The joy of a saint is the most powerful argument for the truth of Christianity.

For many years had flowed by—a dozen or more—from the time when I was nineteen and was stirred by the reading of Cicero's *Hortensius* to the study of wisdom; and here was I still postponing the giving up of this world's happiness to devote myself to the

> **search for that of which not the finding only but the mere seeking is better than to find all the treasures and kingdoms of men, better than all the body's pleasures though they were to be had merely for a nod.** (8/7/17, p. 152)

Through Cicero, God had planted a seed in Augustine's soul. It was like a baptism of the mind. It could not be destroyed or thrown away. No truth, once seen, can forever be forgotten. But it could be, and was, suppressed, ignored, and postponed. Augustine, not Hamlet, is the great procrastinator. (Actually, Hamlet is quite active and decisive.) The eleven years between his first conversion, or his philosophical conversion, and his second conversion, or his Christian conversion, had been a mixture of truth-seeking and truth-procrastinating. The procrastinating was only half of his attitude; the other half was the opposite: the love, the seeking. He finally found the truth (or was found by it) only because he sought it and loved it. For all who seek it eventually are given the grace to find it.

But the long postponing of the active search for this truth was absurd, for the very seeking of this goal (which was implicitly a search for God) was better than finding anything and everything else. This failure was nobler than any other success, this hunger more precious than all other food. C. S. Lewis' autobiography, *Surprised by Joy*, which parallels Augustine's in many profound ways, makes the same paradoxical discovery in his experience: that the mere longing for this ultimate joy, this breaking and blessing of heart, even if the object of this search was unattainable, was more satisfying than the attainment of any other thing.

The reason behind this paradox is the very nature of God. As Austin Farrer says,

> There is nothing, says the scripture, which can be compared with God. It is not simply that he outweighs anything that is weighed against him, it is that nothing can be weighed against him; it is meaningless even to think it. We can compare two of God's creatures, by asking which has more of God in it; if we compare any of his creatures with God, there is no common measure at all. Yet we are always comparing God with trifles, and preferring them to him. We consider whether we shall amuse ourselves, or pray to him; whether we shall obey his commands, or pursue our own game. Jesus let nothing, not his own human existence, weigh against God, he sacrificed it. By his grace we throw ourselves in, to testify that God is all.

> **But I in my great worthlessness . . . had begged You for chastity, saying: "Grant me chastity and continence, but not yet." For I was afraid that You would hear my prayer too soon.** (8/7/17, p. 152)

Once again, Augustine's honesty moves him from the respectable generality to the embarrassing particular: he did not dare to seek the truth because he feared the truth would be Christ, and Christ would demand him to clean up his sex life.

("Chastity" does not mean simply "abstinence from sex". It means simply "sexual virtue", which includes abstinence *for the unmarried* and fidelity for the married. Augustine wanted neither marriage nor abstinence, and he knew Christ would not let him have his third option, "none of the above".)

The search for truth can remain pleasant and comfortably safe as long as the "truth" remains merely theoretical and impersonal. But when it becomes a question of dealing with the living Person of Christ, who with divine authority makes demands on your whole life, with no exceptions, the only escape left is procrastination, which is neither "yes" nor "no" but "not yet". It seems *safer* than either "yes" or "no".

Augustine was wise enough to know his own weakness and addiction, and he knew that chastity could be his only by a divine gift. He also was now wise enough to know that this gift would really be given to him if he really wanted it and asked for it. That's exactly what scared him and why he added "not yet" to his prayer. He realized that if he honestly prayed simply "Thy will be done", he would have to duck—to avoid getting hit with the gift he asked for but didn't really want just yet. Once you invite the Hound of Heaven through your front door, He does not sit politely in the hall. He owns the whole house, including the bedroom.

Augustine is now very close to conversion: for he is scared.

In the torment of my irresolution, I did many bodily acts. Now men sometimes will to do bodily acts but cannot, whether because they have not the limbs, or because their limbs are bound or weakened with illness or in some other way unable to act. If I tore my hair, if I beat my forehead, if I locked my fingers and clasped my knees, I did it because I willed to. But I might have willed and yet not done it, if my limbs had not had the pliability to do what I willed. Thus I did so many things where the will to do them was not at all the same thing as the power to do them: and I

> **did not do what would have pleased me incomparably more to do—a thing too which I could have done as soon as I willed to, given that willing means willing *wholly*. For in that matter, the power was the same thing as the will, and the willing *was* the doing. Yet it was not done, and the body more readily obeyed the slightest wish of the mind, more readily moved its limbs at the mind's mere nod, than the mind obeyed itself in carrying out its own great will which could be achieved simply by willing.** (8/8/20, p. 154)

The great gap between soul and body is no obstacle at all to the soul's control of the body. But the soul cannot control itself even though there is no gap between itself and itself. As Aristotle says, the soul has a despotic power over the body. Unless it is paralyzed, the body has no choice but to obey the soul, despite the radical division between material body and immaterial soul. Though there is a division in nature, there is no division in activity. But within the soul, where there is no such division in nature, there is division in activity, there is civil war and rebellion.

Aristotle explained only part of this paradox when he said that while the soul rules the body despotically, giving it no power of rebellion, the reason rules the passions royally, so that the citizens (the passions) have the power to rebel. But Augustine finds a deeper paradox in himself, for he discovers that this rebellion and division is not only between the diverse powers of the reason and the passions, but also within the single power of the will itself. The spiritual will commands the physical body to move, and it obeys; the spiritual will commands itself to move spiritually, and it disobeys. It disobeys *itself*.

> **Why this monstrousness? And what is the root of it? Let Your mercy enlighten me, that I may put the question.** (8/9/21, p. 154)

Augustine calls this "monstrous" because it seems to disobey the very essential nature of things: nothing can not be itself, yet the will seems not to be itself. This is an apparent contradiction. There are no such things as real contradictions: X is always X and never non-X. Augustine assumes, rightly, that everything has a nature, must be what it is, and acts according to its nature. (The modern mind no longer accepts this utterly logical common sense for one very obvious reason: because if accepted it would impose a "natural law" morality on our sex life.)

Augustine's first assumption, in his first sentence, is that this division within his single power of will is "monstrous". His second assumption, implied by his second sentence, is that to understand a thing, we must understand its origin, its cause. For instance, if God is Man's creator, Man can only be understood as God's image and child; but if mere blind irrational chance is his creator, his nature is random and irrational.

The third sentence shows us the practical working road to a solution. It is passionate prayer, not rhetorical fluff. Augustine really, passionately wants to know, and he is really asking God to enlighten him. He is not talking to us and letting God listen in; he is talking to God and letting us listen in. That is the fundamental reason the *Confessions* is a great masterpiece: because it is not a book, a speech, a sermon, a monologue; it is a dialogue, a prayer, and it is alive, it is made with passionate honesty. No one who prays with such passion and honesty will ever be denied the truth he needs.

> [T]**he mind gives itself an order and is resisted. The mind commands the hand to move and there is such readiness that you can hardly distinguish the command from its execution. Yet the mind is mind, while the hand is body. . . . The trouble is that it does not totally will. . . . For if the will were so in its fullness, it would not command itself to will, for it would already will.** (8/9/21, p. 155)

Here is the answer to the paradox. Nothing in nature can be unnatural, can act contrary to its nature. Dogs cannot be dogless, nor rocks non-rocky. But humans can be inhuman, because they have free will. Animals have only natural animal will, which is one with their instincts, and thus they will always act according to the strongest instinct at the moment. When they are more hungry than tired, they will eat; when more tired than hungry, they will sleep. But man has a will that is influenced not only by his instincts but also by his reason; and this means that his will can choose among instincts. He is like a piano player; the keys are the instincts and the reason is the sheet music. Even when hungry, he can fast, if his reason tells him to and if he obeys his reason.

But his will is not only free to choose among instincts as reason directs but also free to accept or reject reason's direction itself, and this rejection of reason is especially tempting when an instinct attracts him. In other words, his will is divided.

> **Thus there are two wills in us, because neither of them is entire.** (8/9/21, p. 155)

This does not mean schizophrenia, split personality, two selves, two egos, two souls. He has two eyes but not two I's. It is the same single soul, the "I", that both wills and nills, that lives both according to the City of God and according to the City of the World. And at this point in his life, Augustine most deeply loves and chooses his "City of God" identity, even though he chooses it feebly and ineffectively because of his divided will. That is why he prays to God to free him from his sin, not to free him from his conscience.

As the next excerpt says, a divided will is still one will, *his* will, and he is responsible for it all and for its divisions. Augustine at this point has repudiated the false comfort that had been given to him by Manicheeism, which taught that matter and the body are to blame for sin, and thus we, who are "purely spiritual", are blameless.

> **When I was deliberating about serving the Lord my God, as I had long meant to do, it was I who willed to do it, I who was unwilling. It was I. I did not wholly will, I was not wholly unwilling. Therefore I strove with myself and was distracted by myself. This distraction happened to me though I did not want it, and it showed me not the presence of some second mind, but the punishment of my own mind.** (8/10/22, pp. 155–56)

Both the will to love God with his whole heart, soul, mind, and strength *and* the idolatrous will to serve himself and his worldly desires instead of God are his will. He willed both. As he says, this is not "some second mind" or second soul or second self. Each person is a single, indivisible self (that is why he says "I", not "we"—only the demon-possessed say "My name is Legion, for we are many"—), and this single self has a single, indivisible soul and a single body (no reincarnation). And though the organs of the body are divisible (they can be cut into pieces by wounds or death), the powers of the soul are not divisible. Each of us has one reason and one will. But the will is divided, not in its being but in its loves. It loves God as God, and it also loves itself and its own pleasures as gods. It is both monotheistic and polytheistic.

This is not a book of philosophy. But to understand Augustine (and to understand yourself), I think the following philosophical analysis will be useful to many readers.

Sometimes Augustine speaks of our soul's power to love as the "will" and sometimes as the "heart". What does he mean by "heart"? "Heart" in Augustine, as in Scripture, has three distinct but related meanings.

(1) Sometimes it means the source of emotions and feelings, especially the higher, more spiritual and more-than-animal human emotions, including the most central and powerful emotion, love. For love is indeed an emotion, though it is also more than an emotion; it is also a free choice.

(2) Thus the second meaning of the "heart" is the free will, the power of the love that is "charity" or *agape*. This is the love that is commanded by Christ. A mere emotion cannot be commanded, either by another person or even by yourself. You can directly control your choices and actions but not your feelings.

(3) Sometimes "heart" means the non-objectifiable subject, the very "I", the image of the God whose name is "I AM", the mysterious center of our being

> that "owns" all the parts: body and soul and, within soul, reason and will and emotions. It is the prefunctional root of all the functions; the "I" we mean when we say "my" mind, "my" will, "my" soul, and "my" body.

> **Thus I was sick at heart and in torment, accusing myself with a new intensity of bitterness, twisting and turning in my chain in the hope that it might be utterly broken.** (8/11/25, p. 157)

Augustine should not be pitied but complimented for this "torment", this "twisting and turning in my chain". For a prisoner of sin whose chains have not yet been loosed by Christ, there are only two alternatives: surrender or rebellion. Augustine is a rebel. No one can be saved who will not be a rebel. The rebellion cannot of itself succeed, for the power that holds the chains that bind us is too strong for us. But when the slave chooses freedom over comfort and fights against his tyrannical master, this implicit prayer for help will always be answered by the Liberator, who is stronger than the tyrant.

> [F]**or what held me was so small a thing! But it still held me.** (8/11/25, p. 157)

The addictions that bind us (for sin is an addiction: we are all sinaholics) seem enormous and enormously attractive, interesting, and colorful only to the addict. Once the chains of addiction are snapped, even temporarily, the false god reveals its true color: grey. Compare how attractive the prostitute appears to the "customer" before and after. She is "used". She is like a cigarette. Once the worm is eaten by the stupid fish, its true size and importance are revealed compared with the hidden hook.

> **And You stood in the secret places of my soul, O Lord, in the harshness of Your mercy redoubling the scourges of fear and shame lest I should give way again and that small slight tie which remained should not be broken but should grow again to full strength and bind me closer even than before.** (8/11/25, p. 157)

"Where is God?" is one of the most common of complaints. Augustine knows the answer. He is always present, "standing in the secret places of my soul". He is "standing", not sitting or lying down: He is acting. Yet he is "secret", anonymous, quiet, like a tide. The greatest powers are always silent.

The God who is always there and always acting often seems not to be there and not to be acting, not saving us from our miseries, precisely because in not yet saving us from our known miseries, He is saving us from our deeper unknown miseries. Augustine praises Him for "the harshness of Your mercy". God uses "tough love" because "*tough* love" is tough *love*. This is why when we cry for help, He often seems not to answer. He is a fisherman. He is patient. His timing is always perfect, because it is all-knowing; our timing is not perfect because it is not all-knowing.

God's merciful hardness is now "redoubling the scourges of fear and shame" in Augustine's soul instead of diminishing them. Why? What greater evil is God preventing here by not saving Augustine from the lesser evil of his misery? Augustine tells us: the strengthening of the chain of sin. As the conflicted soul gets closer to a wholehearted surrender to God, there is a danger that it may resolve the increasingly pressing conflict by giving up on God and giving in to its idol rather than giving up its idol and giving in to God. As it becomes clearer that it cannot endure the tension indefinitely, the temptation becomes stronger to surrender to the more comfortable, old, familiar habitual sins than to God, even though they are "small things" and He is much bigger. Small things are more comfortable than big things. Analogously, I would not be surprised to find that it is statistically more probable that an engagement is broken one month before the wedding date than six months before. As it gets closer, it can get scarier.

> **Those trifles of all trifles, and vanities of vanities, my one-time mistresses, held me back, plucking at my garment of flesh and murmuring softly: "Are you sending us away?" And, "From this moment shall we not be with you, now or forever?" And, "From this moment shall this or that not be allowed you, now or forever?"** (8/11/26, p. 158)

Is Augustine using "mistresses" literally here or as images for his sins? Perhaps both, for he had both. Note his very Socratic habit of having a dialogue with himself, with his own soul, and even with his own sins. They are so concrete that they can easily be personified. And this can be helpful in substituting something concrete for safer, and therefore more dangerous, abstractions.

> **And now I began to hear them not half so loud: they no longer stood against me face to face, but were softly muttering behind my back and, as I tried to depart, plucking stealthily at me to make me look behind. Yet even that was enough, so hesitating was I,**

> **to keep me from snatching myself free, from shaking them off and leaping upwards on the way I was called: for the strong force of habit said to me: "Do you think you can live without them?"** (8/11/26, p. 158)

Sound seems to us to travel slower as its source recedes from us, or we from it. That is why receding car horns seem to bend from treble to bass. This "Doppler effect" has a parallel in the spiritual realm that Augustine is experiencing here. As he moves closer to God, he hears the call of God more and more and the call of his sins less and less. (This "spiritual Doppler effect" happens to us both before and after conversion.) But he still hears them, though receding, and feels their pleas.

> **But by this time its voice was growing fainter. In the direction towards which I had turned my face . . . , I could see the austere beauty of Continence, serene and indeed joyous but not evilly, honourably soliciting me to come to her and not linger, stretching forth loving hands to receive and embrace me, hands full of multitudes of good examples. With her I saw such hosts of young men and maidens, a multitude of youth and of every age, . . . and in them all Continence herself, not barren but the fruitful mother of children, her joys, by You, Lord, her Spouse. And she smiled upon me and her smile gave courage as if she were saying: "Can you not do what these men have done, what these women have done? Or could men or women have done such in themselves and not in the Lord their God? The Lord their God gave me to them. Why do you stand upon yourself and so not stand at all? Cast yourself upon Him and be not**

> **afraid; He will not draw away and let you fall. Cast yourself without fear, He will receive you and heal you."** (8/11/27, p. 158)

The same concrete imagination that previously held Augustine back from conversion (remember his three great theological problems) now helps him. He concretizes Continence by personifying her as a beautiful woman. And this is not just fantasy, it is true. Continence *is* concrete and personal—and beautiful. He also imagines, with her, many saints who have chosen her over lust, encouraging him to do the same. This, too, is not mere fantasy. It is the real "Communion of Saints".

Saint Thomas says that the only thing strong enough to overcome an evil passion is an even stronger good passion. Sex addicts seldom have a clear picture in their minds of the beauty of Continence, as Augustine has here. They see continence as merely negative, as the mere absence of sex. Similarly, addicts to war and violence seldom see peace as the positive thing it is for Augustine. They see it simply as the absence of war, and war seems preferable because it seems more exciting. (What's more exciting than killing or being killed?)

This is why a close relationship with the Blessed Virgin Mary is so effective an antidote to both of these poisons of the modern world, lust and violence. In her, both chastity and peace become positive and beautiful.

And fruitful. Her fruits are joys. They come from her spiritual Husband, the source of all joy. Her soul is fertilized, impregnated, fructified by God her Spouse. It is of this "spiritual marriage" that physical sex is a pale image. Christianity is infinitely more sexy than our sex-saturated culture.

The Conversion in the Garden

What happens next would change the history of Western civilization. Much more importantly (since civilizations are merely mortal), it would change Augustine's eternal soul.

> [A] **mighty storm arose in me, bringing a mighty rain of tears. That I might give way to my tears and lamentations, I rose from Alypius: for it struck me that solitude was more suited to the business of weeping. . . . I flung myself down somehow under a certain fig tree and no longer tried to check my tears, which poured forth from my eyes in a flood,** ***an acceptable sacrifice to Thee*****.** (8/12/28, p. 159)

Why do we do the very same thing—weep—both when we are in very great pain and when we are in very great joy? Why is water both more terrifying and more delightful than land? Why does the same thing that terrifies and drowns us in floods and hurricanes also give us such a sense of peace? In Scripture water is a symbol of both life ("living water") and death (Noah's flood, the Red Sea).

> **There was a garden attached to our lodging. . . . To this garden the storm in my breast somehow brought me.** (8/8/9, p. 153)

Mankind was created in a garden. Mankind fell in a garden. God was tempted in a garden. A garden is a natural symbol of the private, mysterious center of our soul. Italian houses today, as in Augustine's day, typically have inner gardens, atriums, rather than exterior yards. And now Augustine retreats both literally into his exterior physical garden and interiorly into the very center of his soul.

> **I continued my miserable complaining: "How long, how long shall I go on saying tomorrow and again tomorrow? Why not now, why not have an end to my uncleanness this very hour?"**
>
> **Such things I said, weeping in the most bitter sorrow of my heart. And suddenly I heard a voice from some nearby house, a boy's voice or a girl's voice, I do not know: but it was a sort of sing-song, repeated again and again, "Take and read, take and read."** (8/12/28–29, p. 159)

When Augustine speaks, he simply repeats himself. But when he listens, he hears something new. He cannot save himself; he can only be saved by Another. This is why Solomon, or the anonymous author of Ecclesiastes, ends as he begins, with "all is vanity", while Job ends with the Beatific Vision: because Solomon, like Job's three "friends", talks all the time but Job also listens. Job talks not just *about* God but *to* Him and therefore gets an answer. Augustine is like Job. The whole of the *Confessions* is talking to God rather than just about Him. And therefore it is a *listening*. A very unusual achievement for a book! Its words bespeak a great silence.

Whether the voice that sang "Tolle, lege, tolle lege" ("Take and read, take and read") was a supernatural, miraculous act of God or just the natural voice of a child, it was the voice of God in either case. The author of Providence and the author of miracles is the very same One.

It may seem as if the voice elicited Augustine's listening to it, but in fact it was his listening that elicited the voice. Elicited it, not caused it. God speaks to us at every moment, in "the sacrament of the present moment". But we seldom pay attention. We are all severely handicapped children with spiritual Attention Deficit Disorder. But we are *God's* handicapped children, and He loves us like crazy.

> **I ceased weeping and immediately began to search my mind most carefully as to whether children were accustomed to chant these words in any kind of game, and I could not remember that I had ever heard any such thing. Damming back the flood of my tears I arose, interpreting the incident as quite certainly a divine command to open my book of Scripture and read the passage at which I should open. For it was part of what I had been told about** [Saint] **Antony, that from the Gospel which he happened upon he had felt that he was being admonished, as though what was being read was being spoken directly to himself: *Go, sell what thou hast and give to the poor, and thou shalt have treasure in heaven; and come follow Me.* By this experience he had been in that instant converted to You.** (8/12/29, pp. 159–60)

Augustine is certainly not recommending this as a general practice or technique of discernment. (Imagine someone randomly turning the pages of Scripture to "And Judas went out and hanged himself" and then, next time, "Go and do thou likewise"!) But God occasionally speaks to an individual in a unique and unusual way, such as this; and when He does, He always gives that individual the certitude that He, not just he, is behind it. Especially for a man like Augustine, that certitude is very rare and very clear. Augustine is such a doubter and questioner, and so familiar with uncertainty, that it would be terribly cynical of us to judge him as naïve and thoughtless in believing that this was not just self-deception but God, Who was doing the same thing for him as He had done to Saint Antony. You may mistake the voice of your own soul for the supernatural voice of God; but when God speaks to you supernaturally, you do not mistake His voice for yours.

> **So I was moved to return to the place where Alypius was sitting, for I had put down the Apostle's book there when I arose. I snatched it up, opened it and in silence read the passage upon which my eyes first fell: *Not in rioting and drunkenness, not in chambering and impurities, not in contention and envy, but put ye on the Lord Jesus Christ and make not provision for the flesh in its concupiscences.*** (8/12/29, p. 160)

We seldom see God's hand at work as clearly as we do here. This verse is exactly what Augustine needs. He now reads Scripture, not as a universal and impersonal advertisement addressed to "dear occupant", but as a love letter addressed personally to him and signed personally by God. God always gives us exactly what we need. (God is always exact, never vague.) But we do not always see it. And we can deduce from these two premises the conclusion that one of the things we do not always need is to see it. In fact, one of the things we most need is to live by faith, not by sight.

God does not tell Augustine how to conquer "the flesh". He tells him, through the Apostle Paul, to ignore it ("make no provision for the flesh"), to look at the face of God instead. That is the key to becoming a saint: "the practice of the presence of God". And that is the dress rehearsal for Heaven.

The difference between earth and Heaven is the eyes. In Heaven we will get a new set of eyes, which will let us see God face to face. (If He shone the light of that Face on us now, we would die: "Man shall not see me and live."). In this world, faith is our deepest eye. We have four sets of eyes here, and a fifth hereafter: the Beatific Vision of God face to face. Here, we have (1) external sense perception, (2) reason, (3) the "third eye" of intuition, and (4) faith. Each of these can see what is really there, and each is needed because each can sometimes see what the other three cannot.

> **I had no wish to read further, and no need. For in that instant, with the very ending of the sentence, it was as though a light of utter confidence shone in all my heart, and all the darkness of uncertainty vanished away. Then leaving my finger in the place or marking it by some other sign, I closed the book and in complete calm told the whole thing to Alypius.** (8/12/29–30, p. 160)

This is truly and literally miraculous—as miraculous as the *sudden* stilling of a stupendous storm at sea, as in the Gospel (Mt 8:23–27). Augustine's face had been red, body trembling, pulse racing, pores sweating. All this was the embodiment of the storm in his soul. Then, suddenly, total peace, "complete calm". No human power, but only the creative Word of God, can instantly transform such a stormy state, of the sea or of the soul, into perfect peace. It is the peace "not as the world gives" (Jn 14:27). The Word of God in print is being used by the Word of God in person. The Bible is a sword (Heb 4:12), and it is being swung by the divine Swordsman to pierce the very center of Augustine's restless heart and bring it to its rest.

Christ stilled the storm on the Sea of Galilee with a single word: "Peace! Be still!" The sea obeyed like a dog commanded by its master: "Down, boy!" He did the same thing to the inner sea of Augustine's heart. For He is the creator and designer and master of dogs and seas and human hearts.

In this instant, there is more happening, there is more radical change, there is more new being, and at a deeper ontological depth, than in all the external events in world history. Eternity is invading time. What the angel Gabriel said to Mary's body he also said to every Christian soul: "The Holy Spirit will come upon you, and the power of the Most High will overshadow you; therefore the child to be born [in you] will be called holy, the Son of God" (Lk 1:35). Eternity is entering time. Time has no defense.

New Testaments should come with warning labels.

> [A]**nd he** [Alypius] **similarly told me what had been going on in himself, of which I knew nothing. He asked to see what I had read. I showed him, and he looked further than I had read. I had not known what followed. And this is what followed:** ***Now him that is weak in faith, take unto you.*** **He applied this to himself and told me so. And he was confirmed by this message, and with no troubled wavering gave himself to God's good will and purpose—a purpose indeed most suited to his character, for in these matters he had been immeasurably better than I.** (8/12/30, p. 160)

God gives to every individual without exception what he needs, as a doctor tailors his medicines to the patient's specific maladies. Augustine's medicine was a "downer" ("Down, boy!"); Alypius' was an "upper". Augustine was too strong and wild, Alypius too weak and simple. God used their very weaknesses, which were also their strengths: Augustine's passion and Alypius' humility. And He arranged for those two different medicines, those two Bible verses, to have been stored on the same shelf, one right after the other.

Augustine often confesses his pride, and this is totally accurate. But he also shows his humility here, in noting that Alypius, in his greater humility, was "immeasurably better than I". It takes humility to recognize humility in others and not to notice it in oneself. Pride boasts of its own humility and misses the humility of others.

> **Then we went in to my mother and told her, to her great joy. We related how it had come about: she was filled with triumphant exultation, and praised You who are mighty beyond what we ask or conceive: for she saw that You had given her more than with all her pitiful weeping she had ever asked.** (8/12/30, p. 160)

God is the great economist. With a single stroke He satisfies the deepest needs and desires of Augustine, Alypius, and Monica. He can and does use even a large public event that seems impersonal and indifferent to feed the needs of millions of different individuals. We don't usually see that economy in this life, but we are invited to believe in it ("In everything God works for good with those who love him, who are called according to his purpose"—Rom 8:28). Occasionally He lifts the curtain a little so that we can also see it. That is what He was doing here.

Every Christian mother of a wayward child knows what Monica's "triumphant exaltation" must have felt like.

Notice how God's apparent refusal of Monica's prayer for her son's conversion, a refusal that had been going on for half a lifetime, was really His presence, His action, and His compassion to Monica, not His absence, passivity, or indifference. For she now saw that what He gave her in this moment was incomparably better than what she had asked for for many years.

In Heaven we will all see these perfect strategies of divine Providence and will praise and thank God for answering many of our prayers by apparently not answering them. But we can *rehearse*. We don't have to wait for Heaven to do this, only to see it. We can believe it and practice that faith in this life—the faith that (as Saint Thérèse said) "*everything* is a grace." Even the delaying of grace is grace.

Mysticism with Monica

> **When the day was approaching on which she was to depart this life—a day that You knew though we did not—it came about, as I believe by Your secret arrangement, that she and I stood alone leaning in a window, which looked inwards to the garden within the house where we were staying, at Ostia on the Tiber; for there we were away from everybody, resting for the sea-voyage from the weariness of our long journey on land. There we talked together, she and I alone in deep joy; and *forgetting the things that were behind and looking forward to those that were before*, we were discussing in the presence of Truth, which You are, what the eternal life of the saints could be like, *which eye has not seen nor ear heard nor has it entered into the heart of man*. But with the mouth of our heart we panted for the high waters of Your fountain, the fountain of life which is with You: that being sprinkled from that fountain according to our capacity, we might in some sense meditate upon so great a matter.**
> (9/10/23, p. 178)

Whether this was an authentic mystical experience or not depends on how we define the term. The fact that it followed a clear cosmological map, the fact that it was intellectual, should not disqualify it. But if it was a mystical experience, it was a very unusual one in three ways. First, it was in words, in speech, at least until it reached its end. Most mystics emphasize the radical inadequacy of any and all human language to describe their experience. But words are more powerful sacred agents for Augustine than they are for most of us, especially for most moderns. The second feature is even more unique: the experience is not solitary but shared with another person, and shared in words, in dialogue. The third feature is, as far as I know, unparalleled in human history: the other person was the mystic's mother.

A few days after this experience, to everyone's surprise except Monica's and God's, she died. Notice, in the first sentence of the excerpt, the hindsight with which Augustine confesses his lack of foresight. This is one of the powers of the memory, which Augustine explores so deeply in book 10 (sections 8–25). Like the scene in the garden, when Augustine and Monica both saw that God had given them something better than either of them had prayed for, so here, too, Augustine confesses God's providential timing, which we can sometimes see afterwards but rarely beforehand. God was providing a foretaste of Monica's forthcoming journey to the Heavenly vision that transforms suffering into joy by transforming time into eternity.

Notice also that this joy was not in them, but they were in it. Whatever is smaller than we are, and can enter into us and become a part of us, is of the world and not to be adored as our end but used as our means. Whatever is bigger than we are, so that it has not been conceived by "the heart of man", but we must enter into it, with bowed knees —this is of God, an attribute or property of God, and this is to be obeyed, not commanded. It is our end, not just our means. Truth, goodness, beauty, joy, and charity are five of its names.

> **And our conversation had brought us to this point, that any pleasure whatsoever of the bodily senses, in any brightness whatsoever of corporeal light, seemed to us not worthy of comparison with the pleasure of that eternal Light, not worthy even of mention. Rising as our love flamed upward towards that Selfsame, we passed in review the various levels of bodily things, up to the heavens themselves, whence sun and moon and stars shine upon this earth. And higher still we soared . . . and so we came to our own souls, and went beyond them to come at last to that region of richness unending, where You feed Israel forever with the food of truth.** (9/10/24, p. 178)

Here again, for the second time in the *Confessions*, we find a hierarchical mysticism. It does not simply reject the universe of material things as illusion or valueless; nor does it idolize it; but it uses it as a road. A road is good and meaningful and purposeful; but its purpose is not in itself but in its destination. It is not home; it *leads* home. It is a ladder, and Augustine enumerates and follows each rung:

> first, "the various levels of bodily things";
>
> then, "the heavens", which are higher literally and physically than the earth and therefore a natural symbol of what is higher than any physical thing, even though it is itself physical;
>
> then, the soul, which is higher than the heavens (and elsewhere Augustine specifies also at least six different levels within the soul: life, sensation, common-sensory judgment, reason, memory, and contemplation);

finally, "that region . . . where You feed Israel forever with the food of truth"—a beautiful description of Heaven, which is a "region" or place defined by a relationship, not a relationship defined by a region. Because the relationship is with the One who is not part of the universe, this "region" is not itself part of this universe. It is the relationship with the One who feeds our hungry souls with the only food that can satisfy them, the food of truth, that is, with Himself, both His divine Mind and His incarnate Body.

So we said: "If to any man the tumult of the flesh grew silent, silent the images of earth and sea and air: and if the heavens grew silent, and the very soul grew silent to herself and by not thinking of self mounted beyond self: if all dreams and imagined visions grew silent, and every tongue and every sign and whatsoever is transient—for indeed if any man could hear them, he should hear them saying with one voice: 'We did not make ourselves, but He made us who abides forever': but if, having uttered this and so set us to listening to Him who made them, they all grew silent, and in their silence He alone spoke to us, not by them but by Himself . . . and if this could continue, and all other visions so different be quite taken away, and this one should so ravish and absorb and wrap the beholder in inward joys that his life should eternally be such as that one moment of understanding for which we had been sighing—would not this be: *Enter thou into the joy of thy Lord*?" (9/10/25, p. 179)

The whole point of God giving us such mystical appetizers of Heaven is the same as the whole point of a chef serving culinary appetizers: not to satisfy us, but to stimulate us, to make our hearts not less restless but more.

Augustine treats the "ladder" on which he has ascended —i.e., all created things—neither as something evil (as in Manicheeism) or illusory (as in Buddhism) nor as an end that can bring final peace and joy to our souls (as in naturalism); but as something good as a ladder is good or as a road is good or as a womb is good. All three of these things are good only if we move through them and leave them behind. You can't live forever on a road, on a ladder, or in a womb.

We can rehearse in this life for this "leaving them behind" which will be perfected in Heaven, but only by what Augustine calls an interior "silence". The good and beautiful voices of created things, which are the rungs of this cosmic ladder, each utter their own proper sound as we climb them; and after they sing to us, these voices must grow silent as we move above them. Only when we are at the end of our journey do time and motion cease, and then, in "that one moment of understanding for which we had been sighing", we hear the voice from within the eternal palace whose door we have found (or been found by: "I AM the door") saying: "Enter. Enter into the joy of thy Lord."

This timeless moment lacks nothing good, true, beautiful, or joyful that was in time. It is not so much time*less* as full of time, or, rather, full of all the being that we found in time in a dispersed and broken fashion, but now together. This practical payoff is the existential bite of Augustine's highly theoretical speculation about time and creation in the later books of the *Confessions*.

Insofar as time is merely physical, measured by the movement of bodies through space, the present moment is only a dimensionless point separating past and future. It is able to contain nothing. The past is no-longer, the future is not-yet, and the present is merely the line between these two, if we confine time to objective *kronos*.

But insofar as time is spiritual (*kairos*), it does not measure us so much as we measure it; and here the present does not separate past and future but contains them and brings them together. This is the eternal present, the full present. The present of *kronos* is contained by past and future, but the present of *kairos* contains past and future. Nothing is lost. Everything is transformed: "Behold, I make all things new." Eternity has descended into time in the person of Christ and transformed time into Jacob's ladder. It has straightened out time and made it vertical *kairos* instead of horizontal *kronos*, a ladder rather than an endless circle. This (Christ, the Incarnation) is what Kierkegaard called "the absolute paradox": that eternity got a beginning, a birth in time. This rupture and rapture of time by eternity happened in a stable in Bethlehem, and it also happens in each believing and baptized soul.

If you protest that all this stuff about time and eternity is not clear, welcome to the human race. If it is clear to you, you must be either a mystic or a muddlehead.

And my mother said: "Son, for my own part I no longer find joy in anything in this world. What I am still to do here and why I am here I know not, now that I no longer hope for anything from this world. One thing there was, for which I desired to remain still a little longer in this life, that I should see you a Catholic Christian before I died. This God has granted

> **me in superabundance. . . . What then am I doing here?"** (9/10/26, p. 180)

Monica was Augustine's placenta twice: physically, when she was God's procreative agent of his flesh, and spiritually, when by her love and prayers she was God's procreative agent of the new birth of his spirit. In both cases, once the placenta has done its work, it is set aside, it dies. Once you have climbed the ladder to the roof, you leave it behind. You do not take it up with you. It is like the first stage of a rocket; it exists to propel the second stage forward. When it has done its job, it detaches.

> **What answer I made, I do not clearly remember; within five days or not much longer she fell into a fever. . . . [O]n the ninth day of her illness, in the fifty-sixth year of her life and the thirty-third of mine, that devout and holy soul was released from the body.** (9/11/27–28, pp. 180–81)

Augustine does not tell us, or even remember, what answer he gave to Monica's argument for leaving him. One does not usually win arguments with one's mother. Even Jesus lost at least one argument to His Mother, at the wedding feast in Cana. He is happy to "lose" many more to the same relationship. For that relationship certainly has not been abolished or even weakened by the end of His Mother's earthly life and her Assumption into Heaven. So we would be very wise to take advantage of Heaven's arrangement of motherly resources by our prayers for her persuasive intercession and that of Saint Monica. Surely Augustine was not the only reason God raised her up and trained her in this life in the way of prayer and intercession. She has brought many other mothers' wayward Augustine-like children to grace and glory and will continue to do so again and again until motherhood is no more.

> **I closed her eyes; and an immeasurable sorrow flowed into my heart and would have overflowed in tears. But my eyes under the mind's strong constraint held back their flow. . . . I accused the emotion in me as weakness; and I held in the flood of my grief. . . .** [B]**ut I knew what I was crushing down in my heart. I was . . . ashamed that these human emotions could have such power over me—though it belongs to the due order and the lot of our earthly condition that they should come to us. . . .** [L]**et him read it who will and interpret it as he will: and if he sees it as sin that for so small a portion of an hour I wept for my mother, . . . who had wept so many years for me . . . let him not scorn me.** (9/12/29, 31, 33, pp. 181–83)

Monica's death (and Augustine's reaction to it) is the last important event in the narrative. The *Confessions* is only the beginning of Augustine's life, but it is the end of Monica's. In that sense, the book is the story of her life more than of his.

When we read how hard it was for Augustine to admit and accept his tears of grief, we see how deeply Augustine has been influenced by the pagan Stoic psychology of the repression of emotions. Yet he was not influenced by any of the Stoic heresies, since Christians do not take their dogmas from their culture's natural philosophy or psychology but from their supernaturally revealed theology.

Stoic psychology was an honorable and moral but rigid kind of male chauvinism (has any woman ever embraced Stoicism?). It rejected, as womanly weakness, any giving in to tears, for this was seen as "the divine reason" in us giving way to animal emotion. Augustine's Christian and Biblical rather than pagan anthropology of the heart allowed spiritual emotions to share equal value with intellect and reason. And above all, his supreme model is now, not the ideal Stoic philosopher, but Christ, God Incarnate, who freely wept at Lazarus' tomb and at the hardhearted unbelief of His own people in Jerusalem, where He identified Himself with a mother hen, not a rooster (Mt 23:37). But Augustine's emotional personality at this point has not yet fully assimilated the Christian dogmas that his mind and will have embraced. It takes time for water to sink into the deep roots of a great tree.

The issue of the relationship, or integration, of reason and the passions, or emotions, is one that Augustine never quite resolved, finally and peacefully. It may well be asked whether we with all our modern psychologies are any more successful in doing that than he was. Perhaps we are not meant to resolve that tension in this life. For that tension is one of the sources of the restlessness of heart that is the second most precious thing in the world.

Why Augustine Wrote This Book

"But why am I writing this book?" One seldom meets this question in any modern author. Augustine asks it for at least two reasons. First, his Socratic personality keeps questioning everything. Second, his book is in a sense over now. The important events of the narrative concluded with Monica's death, and Augustine now begins his second philosophical bookend (the first one was the first five sections of book 1). Together, the two constitute a frame for the narrative picture.

> **And even if I would not confess to You, what could be hidden in me, O Lord, from You to whose eyes the deepest depth of man's conscience lies bare? I should only be hiding You from myself, not myself from You.** (10/2/2, p. 189)

There is a deep paradox here. It is the great principle, known in some way to all the religions of the world: that the only way to find our life is to lose it, to give it up, and the way to lose our life is to demand to find it, to grasp it. King Ego has to abdicate his throne.

A more philosophical statement of the same paradox is this: if we consent to be objects to God, we become subjects, we fulfill our destiny as images of God, the supreme subject ("I AM"). But if we insist on playing God and beginning with our "I" instead of His, and if we insist on making God our object (which is a kind of idolatry, since He is not an object but the subject ("I AM") and the transcendent Creator of all objects), we find neither ourselves (since we are not the absolute subjects we claim to be) nor God (since He is not the object we make Him out to be).

A more concrete way of putting the same point: We are images of God; God is not an image of us. He is the projector; we are the movie. We are lit up by His light; He is not lit up by ours.

This is why Augustine "confesses", and why we must all "confess", i.e., let ourselves be found by God and stand in the light of truth: because if we try to hide ourselves from God but not God from ourselves, we cannot succeed in either half of that impossible task. We can only hide Him from ourselves, never ourselves from Him. When we run from the light, we run into our own shadow and disappear. Only when we run toward the light, in love with the light and not with ourselves, do we then become ourselves.

All our lives we are like little children playing peek-a-boo with our Father. To grow up is no longer to delight in hiding from Him but in letting Him hide and letting ourselves be found by the hidden God. Only then will He come out of hiding and let us see His face. Only then can we know Him.

> **What therefore have I to do with men that they should hear my confessions, as if it were they who would cure all that is evil in me? Men are a race curious to know of other men's lives but slothful to correct their own. Why should they wish to hear from me what I am, when they do not wish to hear from You what they are themselves?** (10/3/3, p. 190)

In light of the fact that the *Confessions* is a dialogue between Augustine and God, where do we the readers come in? Augustine writes this book not only to God but also to us, and that complicates the relationship and makes it triadic. Why does he let us in on his conversation with God? We are not God; we cannot know and verify and justify and save and beatify Augustine.

That is his question here, and he is testing our answer to it. He does not want many readers! He does not write for the curious, the gossipy, the voyeurs. They should not read this book until they change their fundamental attitude toward it.

In what, exactly, does this change of attitude consist? It concerns the very structure of all human consciousness, namely, the subject-object relationship. Unless we, like Augustine, want above all to be objects to God, to be known by God rather than to be the knowers of Augustine, we will fundamentally misunderstand the intent and purpose of this whole book, and we will misuse it, even if we are great scholars and great philosophers who understand each point in it.

The personal attitude we take toward it colors everything we find in the book. If our attitude is "vain curiosity", i.e., if we are interested in looking at Augustine through our own eyes or through his, he would say of us that "they have not their ear to my heart, where I am what I am." We must match our mind and purpose to his. He wrote the book to help us look at him and at ourselves only through God's eyes. If that was not your purpose when you first read the book, Augustine would tell you to go back and reread the entire book from that changed perspective. If you actually do that, you will see the difference. The changed perspective is, in a word, prayer. You cannot understand any book unless you read it in the same spirit in which the author wrote it; and Augustine wrote it as a prayer. Therefore we must read it as our prayer. *We will not understand the* Confessions *until we pray it.*

The *Confessions* is like the Bible that way. For both books, our profoundest mind is not in our head but in our knees.

> [T]**hey have not their ear at my heart, where I am what I am.** (10/3/4, p. 190)

The heart is the heart of the matter. Where is our heart? What do we love? Do we listen to Augustine's heart with the ear of our heart, loving absolutely what Augustine loves absolutely, namely, truth? (This is what his "first conversion" consisted of, occasioned by his reading of Cicero's *Hortensius*.) If so, we will hear him. If not, not. For that is he, that is his heart, that is where his identity is, "where I am what I am". Therefore, paradoxically, we will understand Augustine if and only if we do not want to understand Augustine but, rather, want to understand truth and, in its light, ourselves, with Augustine's help. Do you dare to expose yourself to that searching light? If not, put this searchlight book back on the shelf.

Theological Conclusions: What Was This God That Augustine Found?

Augustine ends his story with an appraisal of what he has found and how he has found it.

What was he seeking? God, of course, even when he did not know this. But what is God?

God is truth and God is love. These are the two absolutes that sages, saints, and mystics of all religions seek. They are the two values that brook no exceptions, that are universal, and that are eternal. They go "all the way up" to Heaven; for everything else, "you can't take it with you." Medically dead and resuscitated patients who have had "near death experiences" or "out of body experiences" and come back to tell about it always come back with a new focus, a new perspective: they focus always on these two things. They say that nothing matters in life except truth and love, or understanding and charity, or wisdom and compassion. (The Buddhist terms for them are *prajna* and *karuna*.)

Pascal bases his *Pensées* on four great undeniable truths: (1) that all men seek truth, and not just truth but certainty; (2) that no man can claim to have found it; (3) that all men seek joy, the deep joy that comes only from perfect sanctity; (4) and that no man can claim to have attained it. This is the data of experience that must test all hypotheses that claim to explain human life. No philosophy or religion that denies any one of these points is worthy of our time. Only a philosophy that explains all of them is worthy of our belief.

It is with no doubtful knowledge, Lord, but with utter certainty that I love You. (10/6/8, p. 193)

Augustine confesses that he has found the Lord, and therefore has found certainty in place of doubt. He does not say "proof", but "certainty". Are you certain that you exist? Yes. But can you prove it? Is Descartes' "I think, therefore I am" a logically compelling proof? No, it is not, for it commits the logical fallacy of begging the question, assuming in the premise exactly the thing it claims to prove in the conclusion. That thing is, of course, the "I". Would you consent to be tortured for twelve hours every day for eternity if there were some logical fallacy that you did not notice in whatever logical proof you put forth as certain? If not, then you are not certain. However good the proof may be, it alone does not deliver you from all doubt personally. Even if the proof has logical certainty, it does not give you personal certitude.

But you *are* certain of your own existence. So certainty may be attainable, even if proof is not. Can anyone ever be certain of God's existence? Augustine's bold and academically incorrect answer, to an age almost as full of skeptics as our own, is a resounding Yes. He claims not just certainty but "utter" certainty. How?

His short answer is very subtle, almost tricky. He does not say, "It is with no doubtful knowledge, Lord, but with utter certainty that I know you" but "It is with no doubtful knowledge, Lord, but with utter certainty that I *love* you." Love is the path to certainty.

In Dostoyevsky's *The Brothers Karamazov*, wise old Father Zossima answers the anguished plea of Mme. Hohlokov, a scatterbrained and over-educated middle-aged lady who has lost her childlike faith and now fears death; for if there is no God and no immortal soul, there will be nothing but the flowers on her grave. She wants certitude and hopes to find a proof to understand, but instead she gets from Father Zossima (—and from God!) a task to perform, like an experiment in life's laboratory. The task is love, "active love", love of neighbor as if he is an immortal soul, God's own image, intrinsically valuable. Zossima assures her that if she does this, if she lives as if this is true, she will certainly come to know that it is: "This has been tried. This is certain." Unfortunately, she fails the test, for she can only love "humanity" as a distant, safe abstraction. Zossima calls this "love in dreams" and says "I can say nothing more comforting to you. For love in action is a harsh and dreadful thing compared with love in dreams." It is a costly experiment. It costs your very self. But it works.

The heart must educate the head. Love is the supreme knowledge. To be certain of God, you must love Him. There is no other way.

But what is it that I love when I love You? (10/6/8, p. 193)

Once the purely intellectual question of certainty by purely rational proofs is set aside; once love comes in, displaces the usurper reason, and sits on the throne of the soul; then love's first decree is to invite reason to come back and share the throne. The "what" question, which (as Plato knew) is the essential question of reason, comes back in a new context: not merely "what is God?" but "what is it that I love when I love You?"

Notice *two* key changes. First, the quest now is not outside of love but inside of love; not just "what is it?" but "what is it that I love?" Without that dimension, we will get everything wrong, and the more important the thing is, the more wrong we will get it. That is why we can still do physical science and mathematics very well without love, but we cannot do psychology or sociology or, certainly, religion without it.

Second, Augustine does not merely say: What do I love when I love God? But: What do I love when I love *You*? His theology is relative to his religion, i.e., to his prayer, not vice versa. A theology that does not begin on its knees will never rise to its feet.

Put in theological terms, the change is that the human "I" now relates itself not merely to the divine nature but to the divine Person (or, for Christianity, the three divine Persons); to the "Thou" of the "I-thou relationship". This is not just the best way to do theology but the only right way, for, as Martin Buber says in his classic *I and Thou*, "God is the Thou that can never become an It."

So what *is* this "Thou"? What does Augustine love when he loves God? In classic medieval fashion, he gives three answers. His first answer is "negative theology": God is not any idol, not any creature. For God is absolutely unique. "Michael", the name of the commander of God's angel host, means "Who is like God?" Satan's false answer was "I am." The true answer is: "No one and no thing is." Even the "being" of creatures is not the same "being" as the "being" of God, for His essence is existence and theirs is not. We *have* being; He *is* being.

But it is also true that everyone and everything is somehow like God. The second answer to the question "What is God?" is "positive theology" or "analogical theology": every creature speaks of God, reveals God, expresses some likeness to God, for He made them. All art resembles the artist, and the creation is the greatest of all works of art.

Sometimes the "negative theology" comes first and sometimes the "positive theology" comes first, but the third always comes last. It can be called "superlative theology" or "transcendent theology": God is not any of these finite things, not because He lacks any of their perfections, but because He transcends them. His positivity is the justification for our negativity; His superabundant sunlight is the reason for our blindness. He seems dark to us precisely because He is infinite *light*.

Augustine now quickly but lovingly reviews all of sensorially known creation in order both to deny and to affirm that this is what he loves when he loves God. As Charles Williams says, of everything in creation we should say both "This too is Thou" and "Neither is this Thou."

By the way, Augustine, and the medievals who were his disciples, did *not* ignore or despise creation. That is a secularist lie. They loved it more than any secularist ever did, for it was *God's* creation! But it was not their God.

Not the beauty of any bodily thing, nor the order of seasons, not the brightness of light that rejoices the eye, nor the sweet melodies of all songs, nor the sweet fragrance of flowers and ointments and spices: not manna nor honey, not the limbs that carnal love embraces. None of these things do I love in loving my God. Yet in a sense I do love light and melody and fragrance and food and embrace when I love my God —the light and the voice and the fragrance and the food and embrace in the soul, when that light shines upon my soul which no place can contain, that voice

> **sounds which no time can take from me, I breathe that fragrance which no wind scatters, I eat the food which is not lessened by eating, and I lie in the embrace which satiety never comes to sunder. This it is that I love, when I love my God.** (10/6/8, p. 193)

Nothing else is God, but everything else speaks to us of God, as a sign. We must therefore learn the art of sign reading. We must look *along* things rather than just looking *at* them. They are precious only because they are from Him and for Him, not in themselves; for they are not absolutes, they are only relative. Christians are the greatest relativists; they have only one Absolute. This world is not our home, it is our highway. Everything is a kind of Jacob's ladder, let down from Heaven to us by God so that we can climb up to Him on its rungs. The ladder is so beautiful and fascinating, however, that we linger on it. We are ladder-lingerers. We count the rungs or the molecules, but we are hesitant to climb.

> **And what is this God? I asked the earth and it answered, "I am not He"; and all things that are in the earth made the same confession. I asked the sea and the deeps and the creeping things, and they answered: "We are not your God; seek higher." I asked the winds that blow, and the whole air with all that is in it answered: "Anaximines was wrong; I am not God." I asked the heavens, the sun, the moon, the stars, and they answered: "Neither are we God whom you seek." And I said to all the things that throng about the gateways of the senses: "Tell me of my God, since you are not He. Tell me something of Him." And they cried out in a great voice: "He made us."**

> **My question was my gazing upon them, and their answer was their beauty.** (10/6/9, pp. 193–94)

Augustine had been a lingerer for many years; now he is a climber. He asks each rung of the ladder, each creature, "What are you?" "Are you my God?" "Are you my Home?" "Are you my Maker?" He is like the lonely little bird in the children's story asking every creature it meets, "Are You My Mother?" We are all that little bird, and if we seek, we will find. "My question was my gazing upon them, and their answer was their beauty." If we ask honestly, all creatures will answer honestly, and so will all experiences in our life. The universe is a giant schoolroom. All the teachers and textbooks in that school "cry out in a great voice." But the students are usually deaf, dumb, or distracted.

This entering into dialogue with creatures as if they were persons is no fantasy; it is science! All science, primitive or modern, is the reading of God's art. Art creates; science discovers. Art and science are ultimately one; for whatever (divine) art creates, (human) science can discover, and whatever (human) science discovers, (divine) art has created.

> **Where then did I find You to learn of You, save in Yourself, above myself? Place there is none, we go this way and that, and place there is none.** (10/26/37, p. 210)

God is neither in the universe (that is the error of both pantheism and paganism) nor outside the universe (that is the error of deism), for God is not in space. When we say "outside the universe", we say something self-contradictory, for "the universe" means all matter, time, and space. "Outside the universe" is as self-contradictory as "before time" or "after time". "Before" and "after" are time-words. So "inside" and "outside" are space-words. And God is not *in* space, any more than He is *in* time (except by the Incarnation), for that would make Him finite. And since God is not in space, He is neither inside nor outside the universe. Both pantheism and deism make the same mistake: they judge God by the universe rather than vice versa. They draw a large map (usually circular) and say "this is the map of the universe, and we will use this map to map everything, even God. Is God inside the circle or outside it, or both?" And the answer is: Neither. It is like asking whether justice is in odd numbers or even numbers or whether light comes from the color blue or the color red.

The typically ancient idolatry was objective: God was confused with something in the objective cosmos. The typically modern idolatry is subjective: God is confused with something in the subjective consciousness. But God is no more in my consciousness than He is in space. I have ideas and loves and choices and feelings in my consciousness, and God can be the object *of* my ideas, my loves, my choices, and my feelings, and He can also inspire them and cause them, but He is not an idea or a human love, or choice, or feeling.

The same error is common to both the ancient and the modern idolatries, though they seem so different: not letting God be God; mapping God; making God relative to us, to our consciousness, to its subject-object dualism; trying to locate God in either the subject pole or the object pole of our ordinary human consciousness. We and the world are in God; God is not in us or in the world. We cannot locate God; God locates us. God is not an object of our experience; we are objects of God's experience. The answer to

Augustine's question "Where then did I find You to learn of You?" is only "in Yourself".

When we try to find Him anywhere else, we fail. Or, worse, we succeed—in finding an idol, either objective or subjective.

Job complained, "I go forward, but he is not there; and backward, but I cannot perceive him; on the left hand I seek him, but I cannot behold him; I turn to the right hand, but I cannot see him." For, as Augustine said, "place there is none, we go this way and that, and place there is none." Our entire lives consist in going "this way and that", not so much with our lips as with our concepts and words. Another way of saying the same thing is that our entire lives consist in talking. But only when we are silent and listen can God get a word in edgewise. That is what happened to Job. Job gave up. And then God could show up.

> [A]**ll men do desire true happiness. . . . I ask all men whether they would rather have their joy in the truth or in a falsehood: they reply as unhesitatingly that they would rather have their joy in the truth as that they wish for happiness. . . . I have met many who wished to deceive, but not one who wished to be deceived.** (10/23/33, p. 208)

Augustine is still reviewing his quest. It is a quest for happiness, of course, for all men seek happiness—not just contentment (that can become boring), but *joy*. Joy is to happiness what happiness is to pleasure. But we seek true joy, not false joy; we seek joy in truth. These are the two things mentioned above as the two absolutes that everyone seeks and no one adequately finds—joy and truth—and that is why all of our hearts are restless until they rest in God, in divine joy and truth, in true joy. Augustine wrote: "Seek what you seek, but it is not where you seek it. You seek happiness of life in the land of death, and it is not there" (4/12/18, p. 65).

We can't stop seeking joy, we can't stop seeking truth ("I have met many who wished to deceive but not one who wished to be deceived"), and we can't get either one until we get (or let ourselves be "gotten" by) God.

But if this is true, Augustine finds a puzzle: If we all seek truth, why do we often hate it when we find it?

> **"Why** [then] **does truth call forth hatred?" Why is Your servant treated as an enemy by those to whom he preaches truth, if happiness is loved, which is simply joy in truth? Simply because truth is loved in such a way that those who love some other thing want it to be the truth, and, precisely because they do not wish to be deceived, are unwilling to be convinced that they are deceived. Thus they hate the truth for the sake of that other thing which they love because they take it for truth. They love truth when it enlightens them, they hate truth when it accuses them. . . .** [T]**hey love truth when it reveals itself, and hate it when it reveals them. Thus it shall reward them as they deserve: those who do not wish to be revealed by truth, truth will unmask against their will, but it will not reveal itself to them. Thus, thus, even thus, does the human mind, blind and inert, vile and ill-behaved, desire to keep itself concealed, yet desire that nothing should be concealed from itself. But the contrary happens to it—it cannot lie hidden from truth, but only truth from it.** (10/23/34, pp. 208–9)

We cannot love falsehood itself, as such, any more than our eyes can see darkness itself or our nerve endings can enjoy pain. Yet we often seem to do this, for we prefer falsehood and hate the truth when it is revealed to us by God's mouth-pieces the prophets. Prophets of truth are not usually loved; they are usually martyred. The business of being a prophet is a non-profit business. And when Truth Incarnate told us the truest truth about God and about ourselves, we were so threatened that we crucified Him. How is this possible?

This is a very mysterious question. Here is Augustine's answer. We cannot believe something that we know and admit to ourselves to be false, for we cannot believe that it is both true and false at the same time. We cannot avoid pinning the label of truth onto whatever we believe. But we can willfully move the label. We can move it away from something that we suspect is true but deeply want not to be true, like Christian morality, and move it onto its opposite, which we do want to be true. In other words, our free choice extends to choosing to believe whatever we want to believe. Our motive for believing something can be a dishonest motive: because we *want* it to be true, not because it *is* true. But we need to pacify our ineradicably truth-loving souls by believing, or pretending to believe, that this falsehood is true. Because we thus have a divided will, we also have a divided mind. Deep down we know, or at least suspect, that X is true. Because of the natural law and conscience, there are "things we can't not know". But since we don't *want* X to be true, our will moves our conscious, surface mind to reject X. We are "double minded".

Psalm 139 is a test of our single-minded honesty. Once we realize that God knows everything in us, as the psalm confesses, and that there is no way we can ever hide anything from Him, does this give us joy, or does it rankle us or even torture us? When, instead of trying to shine the light of our mind on God to reveal Him to us, we find God's light revealing us to Him, do we love this or hate this and try to escape from it? Do we rejoice even when what the light reveals is our darkness, our follies, our sins, especially our embarrassingly ugly, nondramatic, non-Promethean sins, like cowardice and lies and sloth and whining egotism? When we confess, "You have searched me and known me", do we thank Him for finding the dust we have swept under the rug? If not, then, until we change our fundamental attitude, we come under Augustine's description: "those who do not wish to be revealed by truth, truth will unmask against their will." If we do not want to *be known* by God, we will not *know* Him. But we will be known by Him anyway. If we do not reveal ourselves to truth, truth will not reveal itself to us but we will be revealed to it willy-nilly. For the human mind "cannot lie hidden from truth, but only truth from it".

That is ultimately the difference between Heaven and Hell. The light of truth shines in both places—it shines everywhere—but those in Heaven love it and those in Hell hate it. Heaven and Hell may even be the same place, but experienced in an opposite way by opposite people. For this world, too, is only one place, but it can be experienced in an opposite way by opposite people. Two people attend a concert or a church service or a battle or a brothel: for one it is a little bit of Heaven, for the other it is a little bit of Hell.

The whole of the *Confessions* is Heavenly, even the Hellish parts; the confessions of Augustine's sins as well as the confessions and praises of God's goodness. All those in Heaven have a total, passionate, fanatical love of truth. If we want to enjoy Heaven, we need to practice that Heavenly art here.

> **Late have I loved Thee, O Beauty so ancient and so new; late have I loved Thee! For behold Thou wert within me, and I outside; and I sought Thee outside and in my unloveliness fell upon those lovely things that Thou hast made. Thou wert with me and I was not with Thee. I was kept from Thee by those things, yet had they not been in Thee, they would not have been at all.** (10/27/38, p. 210)

God is addressed by Augustine under many names: Being, Eternity, Life, Love, Goodness, Truth, and Beauty are seven of them. They are all ultimately one in Him, though they are different in creatures, like a single white light that has been separated into different colors by a prism. The prism is time and space and matter—that is, the created universe.

Augustine here confesses his waste of time: "*Late* have I loved Thee." Malcolm Muggeridge, the late-in-life convert, entitled his autobiography *Chronicles of Wasted Time*. When a man falls in love with a woman, he is sad that he has missed the opportunity to know her during the whole previous part of her life. But the beauty Augustine has come to love is the eternal God who is totally present to all time, including all the times that to us are absent because they are either the to-us-dead past or the to-us-yet-unborn future. But God is there, too. God is "so ancient *and* so new".

The supreme irony is the soul's search for God everywhere except where He is: in the very power of searching that is in the searcher. For we, and only we, in this whole universe, are His image. It is like looking for your head everywhere in the world except where it is, in that hairy ball atop your body that is doing the looking.

In this state, before his conversion, was God present with Augustine or not? Objectively, yes; subjectively, no. "Thou wert with me and I was not with Thee." God always says to us, "Here I am, child." But we do not always say to Him, "Here I am, Father." This is a thing we need to practice here because we will be doing it all the time in Heaven. Here, most of us pray only a few minutes a day. There, everything is prayer. But that ubiquity and universality of prayer can begin now. Tying your shoe can be prayer. Even going to sleep can be prayer. "The practice of the presence of God" has no borders, no limits.

Another part of the irony of Augustine's life is that what kept him from God for many years was his idolatry, his love of creatures as his gods, his absolutes, his hope, the source of his happiness. But these were *God's* creatures! Not only did He create them, but He preserved them in being; He was right there at their heart, giving them existence at every moment. He was not contained in them, but they were in Him. "I was kept from Thee by those things, yet had they not been in Thee, they would not have been at all."

> **Thou didst call and cry to me and break open my deafness: and Thou didst send forth Thy beams and shine upon me and chase away my blindness: Thou didst breathe fragrance upon me, and I drew in my breath and do now pant for Thee: I tasted Thee, and now hunger and thirst for Thee: Thou didst touch me, and I have burned for Thy peace.** (10/27/38, p. 210)

This is an amazing passage. It is on fire. It burns our souls. Notice the violence of the imagery here, one from each of the five senses. Augustine is a violent man. But it is an interior violence, a spiritual violence, a violence against himself, not others. Christ said that "the kingdom of heaven has suffered violence, and men of violence take it by force" (Mt

11:12). We do not attain His peace except by His spiritual warfare. Christianity is a religion of love, but that does not mean that it is not a religion of war. It means that it *is*. Love wars against its enemies: selfishness, shallowness, sloth, indifference, self-indulgence, comfort-mongering. God is not a pop psychologist; God is a warrior. Or as Rabbi Abraham Joshua Heschel said, "God is not an uncle. God is an earthquake." Or as C. S. Lewis said, "Aslan is not a tame lion." Oprah would definitely not be comfortable having Jesus on her show.

How can we "burn" for His "*peace*"? Aren't "burning" and "peace" opposites? Isn't "burning" restlessness, and isn't "peace" rest? Yes. But they go together in two ways. Restlessness leads to peace, and peace leads to restlessness. Each causes the other. The only way to His peace, as distinct from the world's, is that burning. And once the peace of God touches you, you will burn for Him. If you are not on fire for Him, it is not He who has touched you.

Conversion does not still the restless heart. It energizes it. The passion does not decrease after conversion; it increases. The closer He gets, the more His love, which is an infinite passion, rubs off on us. Augustine does not say merely in the past tense "I hungered and thirsted for Thee" but "I *now* hunger and thirst for Thee. . . . I *do now* pant for Thee." Would you describe your attitude toward God as "panting"? No? Then something is missing.

Yes, God's love is passionate. To think of the love that is infinite and eternal within the Trinity, the love that created the universe from nothing, the love that dared to create the free wills that it foresaw would rebel and cost Him infinite pain to redeem, the love that freely stepped into the Hell of Calvary for us—to think of that love as anything *less* passionate than our little drips of temporary passion is like thinking of the sun as less fiery than a match. God does not fall in love as we do, not because He is too cold, but because He is too hot. He does not fall in love because He *is* Love. He does not fall in love for the same reason the sea does not fall into the sea and get wet.

In Luke's Gospel, the resurrected Jesus appears to two of His disciples on the road to Emmaus, but they do not recognize Him. They explain to him why they are so sad: Jesus of Nazareth, whom they had hoped was the Messiah, had been crucified, and now their hopes were dashed. Jesus then showed them from their Scriptures that this was no accident, that the Messiah had to suffer. "And beginning with Moses and all the prophets, he interpreted to them in all the Scriptures the things concerning himself." (What would you give to hear that bit of Biblical scholarship?) Then, after he had supper with them and they recognized him in the breaking of the bread, he disappeared. Their reaction was profoundly Augustinian: "They said to each other: Did not our hearts burn within us while he talked to us on the road while he opened to us the Scriptures?"

He preached the Gospel of the Burning Heart. So does Augustine.

The medieval statuary of Augustine that gave him an open Bible in one hand and a burning heart in the other was not meant to be quirky, but universal. If they made statues of you, would they give you the same two symbols? Or would they give you a smartphone and a pillow?